TO THE DEATH'S HEAD TRUE

When in 1977 three Waffen-SS men suddenly appeared in London to promote a book about the Waffen-SS, there was a tremendous outcry in the press. Sensational allegations about the SS trying to 'whitewash' its infamous past, were followed by a number of letters to the newspapers. These ranged from outright indignation that such murderers should be allowed into this country to a letter from a former British officer who had fought against the Waffen-SS and had always found them brave and honourable soldiers. These extremes of opinion, and the fundamental ignorance about the SS – its origins, activities, responsibility for war crimes and crimes against humanity, prompted me to suggest to Thames Television that they should commission me to make an in-depth study of the whole SS.

ANDREW MOLLO

To the Death's Head True

THAMES METHUEN

A Thames/Methuen Paperback

TO THE DEATH'S HEAD TRUE
ISBN 0 423 00060 8

First published in Great Britain 1982
by Thames Television in association with
Methuen Paperbacks

Copyright © 1982 by Andrew Mollo

Thames/Methuen Paperbacks are published
by Methuen London Ltd
11 New Fetter Lane, London EC4P 4EE
in association with Thames Television
International Ltd, 149 Tottenham
Court Road, London W1P 9LL

Made and printed in Great Britain
by Richard Clay (The Chaucer Press) Ltd
Bungay, Suffolk

Contents

Picture Credits

All photographs are reproduced by permission of the Historical Research Unit except the following, which are reproduced by kind permission of Keystone (Nos 22 and 27) the Imperial War Museum (No 12) Novosti (No 18) and Robert Capa/Time & Life (No 14)

Foreword

This is not intended to be another general history of the SS, of which there are already too many, but an explanation, through the medium of interviews with former SS men, victims of the SS and members of the German legal profession, of the complexities of the SS organization, the peculiar character of the SS, and the degree of complicity of each branch of the SS for the crimes attributed to it as a whole.

The interviews were originally done for the Thames Television documentary *SS 1923-1945* which I wrote, produced and directed in 1980. Although many of the interviews were never used in the film and others edited, I have been very conscious of my responsibility to the interviewees not to distort the sense or meaning of what they said to me, and I alone bear the responsibility for any misunderstandings which may have arisen or may arise in the future as a result of my own interpretation of them.

In a way both the film and book are an appeal for forgiveness.

ANDREW MOLLO
Banbury, 15 June 1981

Acknowledgements

My particular thanks must be due to Thames Television for commissioning me to make the documentary film *SS 1923–1945*, and for making available to me a first-rate team of experienced professional technicians, and the vast resources of this distinguished commercial television company. To the head of the documentary department, Mike Wooller, and my executive producer, Udi Eichler, I am very grateful for their patient pilotage through my first documentary film for British television.

Sue Maconaghy, Gita Sereny, Bernd Wegner and Mike Tregenza all provided me with useful suggestions and sources of information, while Suzanne Melling gave up precious socializing time to type out the manuscript, and I am very grateful to them all.

My thanks are also due to the publishers of those books listed in the bibliography from which I have reproduced extracts, and in particular Heinz Höhne's admirably concise and highly recommended *The Order of the Death's Head*.

Finally I would like to thank all those, whose names appear in the list of interviewees, who so kindly gave of their time and granted us interviews. For the former members of the SS it must have been particularly trying, but having once agreed they all faced the ordeal in a friendly and frank manner. At this point I must also express my gratitude and respect to the Thames Television *World at War* team whose objectivity and integrity stood us in such good stead when we came to follow in their footsteps.

Introduction

When in 1977 three Waffen-SS men suddenly appeared in London to promote a book about the Waffen-SS, there was a tremendous outcry in the press. Sensational allegations about the SS trying to 'whitewash' its infamous past, were followed by a number of letters to the newspapers. These ranged from outright indignation that such murderers should be allowed into this country, to a letter from a former British officer who had fought against the Waffen-SS and had always found them brave and honourable soldiers. These extremes of opinion, and the fundamental ignorance about the SS – its origins, activities, responsibility for war crimes and crimes against humanity, prompted me to suggest to Thames Television that they should commission me to make an in-depth study of the whole SS.

Having assured Thames that such a film was not going to be a whitewash of the SS, the next step was to find a German-speaking researcher who could contact former SS men and convince them that it would be a good idea to appear in a British television documentary film. My final choice for this tricky task was a thirty-four-year-old English girl who had been married to a German and lived and studied in Munich. Not only was Pamela Portugall's German excellent but her attitude open and her approach sympathetic. I felt that if anybody could put these people at ease, it would be Pamela. The wife of one of our SS interviewees didn't take long to see through my ploy, and resignedly said to her husband 'you see they get a pretty girl to interview you, and hope you'll say more than you intended'.

Since the SS was a complex and multifarious organization

it was my original intention to interview at least one SS man from each of the different branches of the SS. It was not difficult to find former Waffen-SS men and anyway I already knew some because of my previous researches on the SS. Generally speaking they are quite willing to talk about their experiences because they consider themselves soldiers first and foremost, and none of them had been accused, let alone found guilty of war crimes.

Our most important contact was the former Waffen-SS Lieutenant Colonel Richard Schulze-Kossens. He had often appeared on British television – mainly in connection with the controversies surrounding the historical works of David Irvine – and had the misfortune to be on a private visit to London when the row broke out in the press over the British launch of a *Pictorial History of the Waffen-SS*, and was deported together with his erstwhile comrades – ex-*SS-Sturmbannführer* (Major) Hubert Meyer and ex-*SS-Brigadeführer* (Major-General) Walther Harzer. Richard is a handsome man over six feet tall and every inch a soldier. He joined the SS before the war and was seconded to the Foreign Ministry and accompanied the German Foreign Minister Joachim von Ribbentrop to Moscow for the signing of the German–Soviet Pact. With the outbreak of war he joined the *Leibstandarte SS Adolf Hitler* and fought in the Polish, French and Greek campaigns and on the eastern front. In October 1941 with the rank of major, he followed in his late brother's footsteps and became an orderly officer at Hitler's headquarters and from October 1942 until December 1944 he was Hitler's personal adjutant. After taking command of the Waffen-SS Officers' Academy at Bad Tolz he was charged with scraping together the 38th and last division of the Waffen-SS to be formed before Germany finally capitulated on 8 May 1945.

Having agreed to give us an interview and having put us in touch with other SS people – he appeared to know most of the leading surviving SS men – as well as former cadets from Germany and abroad who had attended the officers' academy while he was commandant. He was most helpful until he heard through the SS old-boy network that we had advertised in a Munich newspaper for contemporary witnesses for our SS film, and that we had written to a former Waffen-SS officer who had replied to our advertisement and told him that the Majdanek Extermination Camp trial was to form an integral part of the film. We were anxious to be scrupulously fair in our contacts with former SS people and from the outset had told them that the film was about the whole SS and not just the Waffen-SS.

Richard Schulze-Kossens wrote: 'If this report is correct, I must inform you that I am not prepared to give an interview which begins with the events in the concentration camps, which will inevitably stir up feelings against the SS. As an officer in the former Waffen-SS I am not interested in allowing myself to be defamed again in England if our troops are again to be associated with the events in the concentration camps. Our statements which would distance us from such events would only create the impression of a cover-up.... I want to take this opportunity to say how deeply it would offend me to have our troops portrayed once again as a sort of "soldateska" who committed a string of war crimes. As I have already told you, our experiences with the media have always been disappointing, and I myself have only ever received fair treatment in television interviews in the USA.'

I replied: 'From the very beginning, I have always made it clear this film is a history of the SS, *not the Waffen-SS*, but the *whole SS*, and in this context it would be dishonest of me to extol the military prowess of the Waffen-SS while ignoring the brutalities committed by men wearing SS uniform. I, in common with most historians, know that the SS tree grew from a single acorn, and as it grew, its branches sprouted further apart. This explains why one category of SS man could, in all honesty, consider themselves "soldiers like any others", when in reality they were sacrificing their lives for a system which was basically dishonourable. The fact that a number of Waffen-SS men were unfairly treated after the war, and continued to be blamed for everything done in the name of the SS, is also relevant to our story, and will be covered.

'My personal view is that you and all those that I have contacted, know in themselves to what extent they personally were responsible for what went on in their name, and the clarity of their consciences is illustrated by their willingness to appear in the film. The three officers who were so shabbily treated in England in 1977 will now be given the opportunity to have their say, which was previously denied them.'

Although I have never taken too seriously the stories about Odessa (Organization of Former SS Members) as portrayed in the novel and the film THE ODESSA FILE, there certainly is an SS old-boy network, and once someone like Richard Schulze-Kossens decides to help, you find yourself accepted and passed from one former Waffen-SS man to another. After our first research trip to Germany, we returned to London to organize the search for newsreel film and to plan our return to Germany with a nine-man film crew to film the interviews.

We did filmed interviews with five former Waffen-SS men, and talked to a number of others, but by far the most impressive personality was Hans Wissebach. When we arrived at his home in the old university town of Marburg, we were received by a very unfriendly young man who introduced himself as Herr Wissebach's son. Herr Wissebach had been taking a nap when we arrived and struggled to his feet. When fully erect he stood well over six feet tall and in his prime he must have been a powerful man. But today the right side of his forehead shows the scars of a terrible wound and he is totally blind. Unlike his son, Herr Wissebach was extremely courteous and friendly and for well over two hours he gave us a most fascinating monologue about his life in the pre-war armed SS, the bitter fighting on the eastern front in temperatures of 35 degrees below freezing, how he was wounded in March 1942 and just escaped being shot by Red Army soldiers, his eight years as a prisoner of war in the

4

Soviet Union and his return to Germany in 1951, blind and penniless; and how he married his pen-friend and had four children, and re-built his life and his philosophy – he is a conservative – how he eventually went into politics, and how he has never tried – like so many politicians – to hide his Nazi past. In the Government handbook which lists every MP and their careers, his is the only one which included 'former officer of the Waffen-SS'. 'And that is how I conducted my political work in my constituency. I told them "I was formerly an officer in the Waffen-SS, then I wanted to be a General but that was not to be. But Germany still exists and I will again do my utmost for my Fatherland."

'I know two totalitarian systems – the brown from the sunny side, or so I thought, although I should add that the life of a front soldier is not all that sunny, and the red system from the darkest shadows, and I know everything there is to know about totalitarian systems for the rest of my life.'

Gradually Hans Wissebach's son became less hostile and after the interview, while we were having coffee, he mentioned that he had been to college in the United States, but didn't like it, because as a German he had been subjected to stereotyped anti-German prejudices and had even been accused of being responsible for the crimes committed by his father's generation.

Our advertisement in the *Süd Deutsche Zeitung* had brought forward Wolf Sendele who had joined the Allgemeine or General SS in 1932 when it numbered less than fifty thousand men – mostly part-timers. At that time he saw only two choices: Communism on the one hand and Hitler on the other. Sendele represents the early idealism of the SS, but once Hitler came to power and the aristocracy and other opportunists – or 'march violets' as they were called – flooded the ranks of the SS, Sendele soon grew disillusioned and when he tried to expose corruption in his unit he was kicked out. Despite the fact that Sendele had not been in the SS since 1934 and had served throughout the war in the German

5

Army, he was arrested by the Americans in May 1945 and taken with other local Nazis to help clear up the recently liberated concentration camp at St Georgen, a subsidiary camp of Mauthausen. He will never forget and is still much affected by the fact 'that in this camp they had also locked up children, and I feel the Americans were right to make us see it, and this is still my point of view today when people doubt the figure of five or six million [Jews] dead or try and make a comparison with the number of German soldiers who died in the war; or who say that two million Germans died after the capitulation in May 1945, my only reply can be that if it was only the eight children that I saw there it was the greatest shame of all time'.

Finding a former concentration camp guard was not so easy because those that are still living are either in prison or at liberty and unwilling to draw attention to themselves. The International Camp Committee made up of concentration camp survivors promptly replied to our request for names and addresses of former camp guards living in West Germany or Austria, by supplying a list of over a hundred names including a number of women. Poor Pamela sat down in her Düsseldorf hotel room, steeled herself, and began at the top of the list. An hour later we agreed to give up; they had either moved away, or were not interested in co-operating with us. There was one old lady who was obviously dying to talk to us, but couldn't pluck up the courage. Finally after much toing and froing, telephone calls and form-filling Pamela Portugall managed to see former SS Captain Herman Hackmann in Düsseldorf Remand Prison where he had been held since becoming, in December 1975, a defendant in the Majdanek Process. Hackmann was formerly deputy commandant and in charge of the protective custody compound of this camp. Previously he had served at Buchenwald where it was alleged he had behaved like a beast, but in Majdanek 'where murder was as common as coffee for breakfast' he became what the Germans call a *Schreibtischmörder*, or desk murderer, who simply signed the orders which resulted in death by shooting, gassing or injection. After agreeing to be interviewed, he could not face the ordeal and changed his mind.

It looked as if we were going to have a film about the SS without interviews with those most implicated in its criminal activities. However, we found that a West German television documentary director Ebbo Demant had filmed extensive interviews with three former guards from Auschwitz – Erber, Klehr and Kaduk. They are three out of the sixteen defendants who were tried in the so-called Auschwitz Process which started in December 1965 in Frankfurt on Main and went on until 16 September 1966. During his career as *Blockführer* (in charge of a block or hut in which about two hundred prisoners lived) Kaduk murdered either by himself or with the assistance of other SS men or capos at least one thousand people. Of all the sixteen defendants Kaduk earned the unenviable honour of being described as the cruellest, most brutal and most vulgar SS man in the whole of Auschwitz. Erber came to Auschwitz in 1940 and in 1942 was transferred to the political or Gestapo section and was responsible for dealing with the new arrivals that came by train to Auschwitz from all over German-occupied Europe. In his interview he describes how the transports were divided into two groups: those that were going into the camp, and those who were to go into the gas chambers. Erber was found guilty of participating in at least seventy murders. Josef Klehr was a medical orderly in the Revier where inmates who were ill and too sick to carry on working were killed by a lethal injection. Klehr administered some of these injections and was found guilty of murder in at least four hundred and seventy-five cases and accessory to collective murder in at least six cases, two of which involved at least seven hundred and fifty people, in the third at least two hundred and eighty people, in the fourth at least seven hundred people, in the fifth at least two hundred, and in the sixth at least fifty people. His verdict? 'Death by injection was far less cruel than gassing.'

Klehr, Kaduk and Erber conform exactly to the public's

idea of a typical SS man. They are coarse, uneducated, brutal and sadistic. Their crimes defy imagination in terms both of sheer numbers and in the ghastly sordidness of their perpetration and yet, according to the former Auschwitz guard, the late Peter Bock who was made an honorary member of the Auschwitz Survivors' Association, such sadists were in a minority even in the hell-hole of Auschwitz. The majority of the guards had been transferred to Auschwitz and were neither particularly kind nor particularly cruel to the inmates.

Our most important interview was to be with the most senior surviving SS man, Karl Wolff. Karl Wolff had been an officer in one of the oldest and best regiments in the Imperial Army, the Hessian Life Guard Infantry Regiment, and after the Great War he worked as an advertising agent until forced out of business by the slump. Karl Wolff joined the SS in 1931 and embarked on what has been described as a *Blitzkarriere*. In July 1933 he became Himmler's personal adjutant and came to know Himmler 'like nobody else knew him'. In 1939 Himmler sent his *Wolffchen* (little Wolf) as liaison officer to Hitler's headquarters and he remained at the epicentre of power until September 1943 when an increasingly jealous and suspicious Himmler appointed Wolff as Highest SS and Police Leader in Italy. While waging a particularly vicious war against Communist partisans in what had virtually become a Civil War in Italy, Wolff made contact with the Allied secret service and began negotiations which would bring the war to a speedy end. In fact fighting in Italy ceased on 29 April, nine days before Germany's total surrender, thus saving countless lives and much unnecessary destruction.

In recognition of Wolff's role in the Italian capitulation he was not indicted at the International Military Tribunal in Nuremberg but, still wearing his general's badges of rank, Wolff appeared as a prosecution witness on a number of occasions. His conduct both at the end of the war and in Nuremberg has made him many enemies in post-war SS circles, and the Waffen-SS in particular are incensed that this 'salon general' should continue to consider himself a former general of the Waffen-SS although he still does not receive a pension as such from the Federal German government.

In June 1949 Karl Wolff was sentenced to four years hard labour for having been a senior member of the SS, but fourteen days later he was set free because the time he had already spent in prison since the end of the war was taken into account. After his release he built up a successful advertising agency and was able to live with his wife and two sons in a luxurious villa on the Starnberger Sea near Munich – a favourite watering hole of many former Nazi prominents. In 1961 during the Eichmann trial a West German magazine published extracts from Karl Wolff's as yet unpublished memoirs, which led to legal proceedings being opened against him by the Munich judiciary. In January 1962 Wolff was arrested and after a much-delayed ten-week trial was found guilty and sentenced to 15 years' imprisonment and ten years' loss of civil rights for complicity in the murder of at least three hundred thousand Jews. The evidence for the conviction on this charge was the discovery of a letter in July 1941 from Wolff to the German Minister of Transport Theodor Ganzenmüller in which he reported that 'I have heard with particular pleasure that every day for the last fortnight a train containing five thousand members of the chosen race has made the journey to Treblinka and that we are now in a position to carry out expeditiously this moment of population.' Wolff denied having written the letter himself, and said he did not know that the chosen people were being slaughtered and not resettled!

In 1972 he was interviewed by Thames Television for their much-acclaimed and remarkably objective series *World at War*, in which he described how he had accompanied Himmler on a visit to an *Einsatzgruppe* near Minsk in August 1941, and together they had watched a mass execution. Himmler got too near the mass grave and was splattered with the brains of one of the victims. Wolff had to steady

Himmler, who was on the verge of fainting, and prevent him from collapsing in front of his men.

We were not out for such sensational revelations. To us he was the last high-ranking SS leader and a man who possessed considerable courage and charm. We wanted him to try and explain how it was that a man of his background and upbringing could have allowed himself to become a key figure in such an organization as the SS, and the 'eyes and ears' of such a man as Heinrich Himmler with whom he had absolutely nothing in common. Did he feel that the ideals and conduct of the SS were compatible with his honour as a guards officer? Since he had appeared as a witness in a number of war crimes trials, and had been the defendant in his own trial and had plenty of time to ponder during the long years of imprisonment, I felt he owed it to his own generation and to those that follow him to show his innermost feelings as a fallible human being, not in the context of any single event but in relationship to his moral standpoint.

I still don't think he understood the essence of the question or possibly he thought we were trying to trick him into making another sensational revelation, and he was damned if he was going to incriminate himself for the edification of the British television viewer. The morning's interview was almost a complete waste of time and so we broke for lunch. Pamela and I discussed how we would proceed in the afternoon. We agreed that if he continued to ramble on without getting to the heart of the question, we would get tough and confront him with the Ganzenmüller letter. This is in fact what happened but it didn't really change anything. Wolff, by now getting very tired, embarked on a long self-justificatory monologue which was not what we were after either.

Towards the end of a really sad day in which I had sincerely tried to give him the opportunity to let us into his soul and earn our understanding and even possibly our compassion, I saw him in an unguarded moment slumped in his chair with a look of utter resignation and loneliness in his eyes and I felt sorry for him.

10

To see the SS from the other side of the fence so to speak, we were anxious to interview a former concentration camp inmate, and here we were remarkably lucky in the choice of the Austrian Hermann Langbein, Secretary of the International Camps Committee which is based in Vienna.

Langbein was a member of a group of Austrians who had fought with the International Brigade in the Spanish Civil War and when it ended he was interned. When in the summer of 1940 Germany and Spain shared a common frontier the Austrians were handed over to the German occupying army in France. Langbein arrived in Dachau in May 1941. He will never forget his first roll-call. When all the inmates were drawn up in the *Appellplatz* the order 'caps off!' was given and as thousands of hands snatched at thousands of caps, the pre-dawn darkness was lit up for an instant by the brightness of thousands of shaved heads.

In August 1942 Langbein joined a group of German inmates which was sent to Auschwitz to help combat an outbreak of typhus which had struck without discriminating between the SS and the inmates. Langbein became a clerk and spent day and night typing out death notices. Later he became clerk to the chief medical officer at Auschwitz, Dr Eduard Wirtz. Langbein reminded us that the camp doctors were the only academics on the camp staff, and while some of them, like Doctors Mengele and Entress, were anti-Semites and worked willingly in the murder system, there were others like Wirtz who tried whenever possible to alleviate the suffering around them. By the judicious use of his Viennese charm and by insisting on addressing Wirtz as 'Herr Doktor' instead of using his SS rank, Langbein feels he was able to exert a tiny but very important civilizing influence on him.

While Langbein is bitterly against any tendency which romanticizes or glorifies the achievements of the Waffen-SS, and considers that the Waffen-SS claim to have had nothing to do with the concentration camps as a downright lie, he is equally adamant that one can only judge a former SS man on the basis of his personal conduct. 'My personal feeling, and it is not mine alone, is that someone who was once in the SS must not be made to bear the "sign of Cain" on his back for the rest of his life, and be told "you are an outcast". There are people who joined the SS very young because their fathers sent them, or because as so often was the case with us, the father ruled with an iron hand. Others because they were inspired by a beautiful uniform, and then slid into the whole terrible business, and then it is very difficult to stand up and object – I understand that only too well.'

To investigate in detail the verdict of collective guilt handed down at Nuremberg, and legal status of the former SS man in the German Federal Republic, we interviewed a number of people in the legal profession who were involved in the more recent trials. They all informed us that the concept of collective guilt had been totally rejected as a concept which has no place in democratic law. In England, however, the Nuremberg judgement still seems to carry a lot of weight, and may be considered to have been the very justification the Labour Government needed to deport the three Waffen-SS officers from England in November 1977.

The great expert on 'Operation Reinhard' is undoubtedly Alfred Spiess, Senior Chief State Prosecutor at the State Court in Wuppertal.

Spiess's invaluable contribution was to the understanding of why SS men were never punished for refusing to carry out orders involving the shooting of civilians or who demanded to be transferred away from a death camp as soon as they found out what was actually going on. It transpires that this was because such orders and such activities were illegal according to German military law which was also valid for the SS and Police. Therefore, they could not be put on trial and were simply posted to another unit, although they themselves had been led to expect much severer punishment and possibly even death.

12

The SS from 1923 to 1933

*We carry the death's head on our black caps as
a warning to our enemies, and as an indication
to our Führer that we will sacrifice our lives for
his concept.*

ALOIS ROSENWINK
Organiser SS Headquarters

The early history of the SS, which in just under a quarter of
a century grew into a complex organization numbering well
over a million men responsible for, amongst other things, the
Police, the Concentration Camps and a party army which
effectively became the fourth branch of the German *Wehrmacht*, as written in National Socialist publications, suggests
that it was formed simply to provide Hitler with a small,
highly mobile and thoroughly reliable bodyguard.

This is certainly true as far as it goes, but it fails to explain
why Hitler needed a bodyguard, nor why it could not have
been provided by one of the existing para-military groups at
his disposal. To discover the real reasons one must first look
at the history of the SS's parent organization, the SA.

The first organized body of Hitler followers came into
existence in early 1920 and was called the *Ordnertruppe*,
literally Steward Troop, and its task was to keep order at
indoor political meetings. The *Ordnertruppe* soon became
known as the *Saalschutz* and although it was part of the larger
Athletic and Sports Section of the NSDAP, it was the real
forerunner of the SS, and was already carrying out the
specialized role of guarding speakers.

The Athletic and Sports Section of the NSDAP or SA

13

had come into existence in Munich to replace the Bavarian Free Corps or *Einwohnerwehren* which were being dissolved in accordance with the terms of the Versailles Treaty. A number of *Freikorps* officers including Ernst Röhm and Captain Ehrhardt, while making themselves available to organize and train the SA, succeeded in transforming it from the political arm of the NSDAP into a semi-clandestine military organization along *Freikorps* lines.

Meanwhile the tiny *Saalschutz* based on the *Hofbräuhaus* in Munich owed allegiance to no one but Hitler, and fought for him unconditionally, often against considerable odds. The schism which would eventually lead to an open conflict between the SA and SS was already apparent.

In March 1923 Hermann Göring was made commander of the 1,000–strong SA, and he immediately set up a hand-picked guard detachment called the *Stabswache*. In May its personnel were incorporated in Josef Berchtold's Assault Troop (*Stosstrupp*) Adolf Hitler which initially numbered a mere one hundred men. Thus these four successive detachments – *Ordnertruppe*, *Saalschutz*, *Stabswache* and *Stosstrupp Adolf Hitler* were all forerunners of the SS, and had already developed their own identity, discipline and esprit which was far more pronounced than that of the mass of the SA.

Following the abortive November 1923 Munich putsch the NSDAP was banned and its various formations – including the *Stosstrupp* – were disbanded. Hitler was imprisoned and the NSDAP broken up with many party members going into exile.

On 27 February 1925, after Hitler's release from Landsberg Prison, the NSDAP was reformed and the remnants of the SA which had been held together by Ernst Röhm during Hitler's imprisonment took to the streets once more. In April the former *Stosstrupp* member and Hitler bodyguard Julius Schreck was ordered to form a new *Stabswache*. In May Röhm resigned from leadership of the SA because of differences with Hitler concerning the future role and character of the SA. For over a year the SA, with no central command, fell

14

under the influence and control of the regional party (*Gau*) leaders.

Throughout 1925 the SA was increasingly falling under the control of the party bosses, while its frustrated ex-officer leaders failed to develop any political motivation. They saw the SA as a means of continuing their military careers, and as a future replacement for the *Reichswehr*. In September Schreck requested all party cells to form an SS. On 9 November 1925 the *Stabswache* was officially named the *Schutzstaffel* or SS and Josef Berchtold was confirmed as the first *Reichsführer*. At the same time the new SA leader, Captain (ret.) Franz Pfeffer von Salomon declared the SS to be an independent organization alongside, but subordinate to, the SA and he fixed the size of an SS squad at one leader (*Führer*) and ten men.

The SA tended to mistake SS numerical inferiority and strict discipline for weakness, and delighted in giving the SS the more irksome tasks like selling party newspapers, bill-posting and canvassing new members, but the SS swallowed its pride and continued – even at this early date – to behave like an elite.

In September 1927 SS Order No. 1 instructed SS men not to become involved in discussions at party meetings, and that discussion evenings were for the purpose of political instruction only, during which SS men should not smoke, nor leave the room until the lecture was over. SS men and their leaders were to keep aloof from inter-party squabbles, and should criticism be voiced in a small gathering, SS men must immediately and quietly leave the group with the curt comment that the SS carries out Adolf Hitler's orders. An SS unit assigned to guard a speaker at a party meeting was to form up in two ranks so that dress and passes could be checked before entering the hall. Each SS man must at all times carry his NSDAP membership card, his SS card and the SS songbook. Since the SS was anxious to promote an impression of legality and order, it was forbidden to carry arms, so the leader had also to see that none of his men had concealed 'matchboxes' (pistols) or 'india rubbers' (coshes) on their person.

Although mostly unemployed, SS men were expected to provide their own uniforms which also differed from those of the SA. SS men wore the brown shirt but, unlike the SA, they had a black cap adorned with a silver death's head, a black tie and black breeches, and the swastika armband was edged in black. The right to wear the swastika armband was withdrawn from SS men who had infringed minor regulations.

In special recognition of the SS's steadfastness and loyalty and to confirm its pedigree as direct descendant of the *Stosstrupp*, Adolf Hitler entrusted the SS with the Nazi Party's most sacred relic – the 'Blood Flag' which had been carried at the head of the column which had marched on the Feldherrnhalle during the Munich putsch. It had been soaked in the blood of the sixteen National Socialists (five of them from the *Stosstrupp*) who had been killed by the police volley which had broken up the march.

In January 1929 a new Reich Leader was appointed for the two hundred and eighty strong SS. His name was Heinrich Himmler and his main claim to fame was that he had carried the Reich War Flag at the Munich War Ministry during the 1923 Munich putsch. He was twenty-nine years old and had been a thorough and diligent worker for the Nationalist Socialists in Upper Bavaria.

1930 was a difficult year for the NSDAP and the SA in particular. The differences between Hitler, who saw the SA as an instrument of political struggle, and its chief, Pfeffer, who saw it as little more than an unarmed assault force, came to a head. In the run-up to the 1930 elections the Prussian SA was on the verge of starvation and seething with resentment. Under the command of SA Deputy Leader East Stennes, the SA invaded Goebbel's offices on the night of 29 August, and although technically under Stennes's command the SS guard barricaded itself inside. The SA broke down the doors and beat up the SS men. On 30 August 1930 Pfeffer von Salomon resigned.

At the end of 1930 SS strength stood at 2,727 and Himmler

had already begun to put his racial and elitist theories into practice. The German aristocracy was feeling decidedly insecure in republican Germany. The Army was only a shadow of its former self with neither money nor prestige. Although Prince August Wilhelm of Prussia was wearing the brown shirt, the SA was nothing more than a proletarian rabble. The military snobs who were looking around for a uniformed niche turned to the SS, no doubt partly convinced by Himmler's claim that the SS were the Guards of the Nazi Party, whereas the SA was just the infantry of the line.

In April 1931 the second Stennes revolt once again highlighted the deep-seated resentment felt by the bulk of the SA membership at what they saw as Hitler's faithlessness and the inefficiency and corruption of the party leadership. Once again the plot fizzled out for lack of money, and Stennes's men began to desert him. As before the SS remained loyal to the person of their Führer, and Hitler in gratitude paid the Berlin SS the supreme compliment 'SS Man, your honour is loyalty' which became in due course the SS motto.

By the late summer of 1931 the SS had grown to 10,000 men and was organized as follows: Hitler was now Supreme Leader of the SA, while the day-to-day command was, since January, again entrusted to Ernst Röhm. One of Röhm's most important subordinates was his personal friend, Heinrich Himmler, whose chief of staff was Josias *Erbprinz* zu Waldeck und Pyrmont, a scion of one of Germany's most illustrious princely houses. The SS headquarters was known as the *Reichsführung-SS* and it was divided into five departments or *Ämter*. Department I consisted of four sections: (a) management, (b) recruitment, (c) security service (Heydrich) and (d) finance. Department II dealt with (a) personnel and (b) training. Department III handled legal matters, and IV (a) equipment, press and sport, (b) medical, while V was responsible for special SS motorized and flying units. In June–July Germany was divided into eight SS districts (*Gruppen*) and thirty-eight Foot Regiments. On 31 December 1931

17

Himmler set up the SS Race Office to establish and maintain the racial and ideological purity of all SS members.

Thirty-one-year-old Karl Wolff, who joined the SS in October 1931 and rose to pre-eminence as Himmler's personal adjutant, is today the most senior surviving SS officer. He was typical of many young men from good families whose chosen career in the Army had come to an end with Germany's defeat at the end of World War I, and professions collapsed with the economic slump. Wolff was advised to join the SA, but when he applied he was told 'a big blond fellow like you should join the SS'.

'When I joined the SS as an unpaid volunteer in October 1931 I didn't have a clue about the SS, and knew nothing about the *Reichsführer-SS* Heinrich Himmler. I first met him three months later during a course at the Reich Leadership School in Munich (this was the one and only course attended by the SS as a sub-division of the SA). As the most senior SS leader Himmler made speeches, and it was then that I was introduced for the first time to SS psychology and concepts and also to Himmler's potty ideas. This was in January/February 1932.

'My first impression of Himmler was a great disappointment. I was considerably taller than him and had already been awarded the Iron Cross first and second class, and I had been an officer in one of the best and oldest regiments of the German Army – the Hessian Lifeguard Infantry Regiment in Darmstadt. On the other hand Himmler had no war decorations and had nothing in common with the front soldier; his whole bearing was rather sly and unmilitary, but he was very well read and tried to engage our interest with his acquired knowledge, and to enthuse us with the tasks of the SS.'

Wolff claims that most people who joined the SS at this time had much the same outlook.

'They were deeply disappointed at losing the war, and the ensuing consequences which on the basis of the so-called "war guilt lie" held Germany to be the only guilty party.

18

They were very dissatisfied with the Weimar Republic which did nothing to refute this lie, but on the contrary seemed to be completely acquiescent. They felt, quite rightly, that their own economic future, and that of their families, depended on that attitude being changed, and that it is why the majority of them joined, like myself, in an honorary capacity. With the exception of a few senior leaders we didn't receive any payment, nor were we compensated for loss of earnings incurred in travelling to meetings. They were idealists.'

On 1 February 1932 Wolf Sendele joined the SS (No. 47449) and well remembers the activities of this unit:

'There was continuous electioneering at that time – not like now every few years – practically the whole time from '30 to '33 there were elections in which Hitler was very active. We then had the job of providing security and seeing that nothing happened to the Führer – that he came to no harm.

'Sometimes it seemed as if we were on the go every day – after we'd finished work – we would go off to some meeting or another, often way out of town to the outlying villages near Heidelberg. There were also some Communist-dominated villages where it was pretty difficult to get the upper hand, and so obviously people had to go along who wouldn't turn and run as soon as the Communists told them to clear off.

'I remember one particular meeting held by a Communist Member of Parliament. We'd planned to break up this meeting, but we were the ones to get busted. We were just thrown out of the hall – our feet hardly touched the ground – and landed in the street, drummed out.

'The other Centre and German-National Parties were quite happy to see us beating up the Communists. After all we were doing their dirty work for them. They could have done it themselves – not with punch-ups – but they could have cut the ground from under their feet by getting the unemployed off the streets but they were too genteel for that. The German Nationals, Hugenberg and the like and the *Stahlhelm* (Veteran's Organization later incorporated into the

19

SA), were too fancy to beat up the Communists in the street – they left that to us.'

In April 1932 the escalation of political violence during the run-up to the elections led to the banning of political uniforms, but SA and SS units still paraded provocatively through the streets either stripped to the waist or dressed in white shirts. The bands continued to thump out their stirring tunes and over the heads of the marchers bobbed signs proclaiming 'Uniforms banned but the Spirit lives on'. Shortly after the ban was lifted on 14 June one of the most violent street battles of all broke out in the Communist-dominated working class suburb of Hamburg. When Altona's 'bloody Sunday' came to an end nineteen persons had been shot dead and two hundred and eighty-five wounded. This was to be the climax of the period which was to become known in Nazi chronicles as the *Kampfzeit* (period of struggle) during which fifteen SS men had been killed.

Sicherheitsdienst and Gestapo
1931–1939

*Here nothing, not even the tiniest egotistical
with that a man might have, is not known to
the Gestapo.*

H. HIMMLER

1931 was a critical year in the run-up to power of the Nazi
Party. The already tense political scene had been aggravated
by the world economic slump, and as the unemployed swelled
the ranks of the radical parties, their bitterness brought about
an escalation of political violence which pushed Weimarian
Germany to the very brink of anarchy and revolution.

Himmler's tiny SS – still subordinated to the SA – found
the task of guarding Hitler and other Nazi speakers increasingly difficult. The SS could not simply sit and wait for
attempts on Hitler's life, nor permit powerful political
alliances to emerge in opposition to the NSDAP, nor was
Himmler willing to see his precious SS trampled on in a
scramble for power within the Nazi Party itself. He decided
that it was time the 10,000-strong SS had its own intelligence
service, but so little did Himmler know about such matters
that he interviewed a young naval signals officer (*Nachri-
chtenoffizier*) in the mistaken belief that he was an intelligence
officer (*Nachrichtendienstoffizier*). Twenty-seven-year-old
Reinhard Tristan Heydrich had recently been dismissed
from the Navy, was unemployed and far from home, so he
was disinclined to explain to the *Reichsführer* the difference.

Himmler accepted Heydrich's draft proposals for setting

21

up an SS intelligence service and, after a short spell of duty in the ranks of the Hamburg SS, Heydrich returned to Munich in August 1931 to begin work. On a kitchen table, with a borrowed typewriter, a pot of glue, scissors and some files, Heydrich, now leader of the Security Service (*Leiter des Sicherheitsdienstes*), aided by his landlady and some out-of-work SS men, began to gather information on what the Nazis referred to as the 'radical opposition'. Top of the list were the political churches, Freemasons, Jews and Marxists. A titillating side-line was homosexuality and 'mattress affairs' both inside and out of the Nazi Party. Heydrich then toured the SS regional commands throughout Germany, and on his return began to recruit men of his own age and background into the SD. In contrast to the typical Nazi '*Lumpenpack*' Heydrich sought bright young university graduates whose career prospects had been dimmed by depression. It was these young intellectuals from good families who were to give the SD its peculiar character.

At the beginning of September 1931 SS regional commanders were secretly ordered to set up an Ic* desk in their headquarters, but this decentralized system of intelligence-gathering by SS men with no experience or special training led to a number of embarrassments for Heydrich, and he was obliged to set up an independent SD chain of command.

In April 1932 the SA and SS were banned and Heydrich had to go underground. His embryo intelligence service became the Press and Information Service, but the ban was only one of Heydrich's many problems, the most acute of which was a desperate shortage of cash. He himself received a pittance and all he could give his helpers was a bowl of soup, while the telephone of the *Zentral* in Munich Nymphenburg was often disconnected because the SD couldn't pay its phone bill.

Another temporary set-back to his rapid rise in the SS hierarchy was the charge made by the *Gauleiter* of Halle-

* Ic was the German military designation for the department in the General Staff which dealt with information concerning the enemy.

Merseburg (Heydrich's birthplace) that there was Jewish blood in the Heydrich family. The charge was never conclusively proven and anyway Heydrich was already too important to dismiss. The embarrassing claim was swept under the carpet, but many of his contemporaries and some post-war historians have linked Heydrich's fanatical anti-Semitism and raging inferiority complex to his Jewish ancestry. However, less than a year later all these problems were overtaken by events, when in March 1933 Adolf Hitler came to power.

When the euphoria subsided it seemed as if the SS had been overlooked. Himmler was not rewarded with a ministerial post, and the SS watched quietly from the sidelines as many plum positions of power were filled by 'March violets', opportunists who as often as not were not even members of the NSDAP. Himmler, however, did not appear unduly perturbed and together with Reinhard Heydrich he began to carve out a role for the SS which would make it, in a very short time, the most powerful and feared formation of the NSDAP.

It is not known whether it was Heinrich Himmler or Reinhard Heydrich who first realized that the path to power lay with the German police, but in 1933 they both began to manoeuvre with such energy that in just over a year the police was firmly under SS control, although it was not until June 1936 that this state of affairs was officially recognized and Himmler was appointed *Reichsführer-SS* and Chief of the German Police in the Reich Ministry of the Interior.

The first step in the process was Himmler's appointment on 9 March 1933 as Acting Police President of Munich by the Nazi State Governor of Bavaria, Franz Ritter von Epp. On 1 April 1933 Himmler became Commander of the Bavarian Political Police and Heydrich took over the political desk of the Munich Criminal Police.

Each of the sixteen *Land* police forces of the Weimar Republic was commanded by a Police President and had its own organization, regulations and uniforms. The Ministry of the Interior in Berlin was the Reich authority but had no executive control over the police forces, other than in the drafting of legislation. The SS saw the inherent difficulties in imposing Hitler's will on these police forces and realized that a national police force was an essential lynch-pin in future in a Führer state.

The story now switches from Munich, the capital of the Movement, to Berlin, the centre of Prussian and Reich government. Berlin was the personal fief of one of Hitler's oldest and most formidable followers, Hermann Göring. He had been appointed Prussian Minister President with commissary powers on 17 February 1922 and immediately set about crushing all opposition with characteristic ruthlessness. Göring loathed the prim and servile *Reichsheini*, although one of his trusted cronies was the commander of the Berlin SS, Kurt Daluege. Daluege's Berlin SS was a law unto itself, and Daluege was damned if he was going to surrender any of his considerable powers to that Bavarian chicken-breeder Himmler. Berlin was not a friendly place for the young SS men from Munich.

On 30 January 1933 Göring was made Prussian Minister of the Interior and began to make a fundamental change in the role of the Prussian Political Police. Forthwith it ceased to be an agency for the protection of the State, and instead became an offensive instrument which enabled Hitler to destroy all opposition and impose his will on the German people. The first step in the formation of a Nazi secret police was the removal of Department 1a, thirty-five staff of the Prussian State Police which dealt with opposition to the Republic, were moved from the Berlin police headquarters to its own building on the Prinz Albrecht Strasse and the appointment of a young jurist, Dr Rudolf Diels, as its chief. On 26 April 1933 this department became the Secret State Police (*Geheime Staatspolizei*) or Gestapo for short. The Gestapo began to be enlarged and reorganized so that it could 'deal with political police tasks in parallel with or instead of normal police authorities'. In each government district (*Regierungsbezirk*) a Gestapo regional office (*Staatspolizeistelle*) was established, first subordinate to, and later independent of, the local government representative (*Regierungspräsident*). The next step was the Gestapo law of 30 November 1933 which made it independent and responsible for all executive functions previously carried out by the Ministry of the Interior. Finally, in March 1934 the Gestapo was separated from the State administration and left with a free hand to carry out its executive tasks as ordered by the Minister President of Prussia (Göring), without further interference from the civil authorities.

Between March 1933 and June 1934 the SS gained control of all the *Land* police forces, and Nazis were appointed to the important post of Police President. By February 1934 only Prussia and Schaumburg-Lippe remained outside SS control.

But Göring with typical astuteness realized that the time had come to improve relations with Himmler's SS and Heydrich's SD, because he could see that Hitler's regime was facing a grave crisis. The problem lay with the rank and file of the Nazi Party which had brought Hitler to power. The brown-shirted SA now numbered over four million men. They had fought with their bare hands with the Communists during the so-called 'Period of Struggle' (*Kampfzeit*), while the SS had faithfully protected their *Führer* from the brickbats and cudgels of the radical opposition in Germany's beer-halls, and yet they went unrewarded. There was nothing now for these 'beer-hall heroes' to do because what Hitler needed more than anything else was brains not brawn.

On 24 April 1934 Göring appointed Himmler Inspector of the Prussian Secret State Police and Reinhard Heydrich its commander, and now the whole police apparatus was firmly in SS hands.

There is no doubt that Hitler felt an emotional debt to his old SA comrade Ernst Röhm, but he could not risk antagonizing the *Reichswehr* generals who, with a mere 100,000 men under their command, felt threatened by SA military aspirations. Röhm's removal would benefit too many people; Göring would rid himself of a rival, the Nazi Party of a political and moral embarrassment, and the SS of subordination to the SA.

At the end of April 1934 egged on by Heydrich and with a powerful ally in the expansive form of Hermann Göring, Himmler began to act. While he toured SS units up and down the country and briefed their leaders, Heydrich's SD began compiling lists of victims, and searching for proof of an imminent SA coup, which was not so easy, since none was planned. Although primarily aimed at the leadership of the SA, it was not long before the purge became a general clean-up and the death lists grew longer and longer.

While the whole operation, including Hitler's role in it, was carefully orchestrated by Göring, Himmler and Heydrich, the executive tasks were dealt with by the Gestapo and the armed units of the SS. When the shooting died down early in the morning of 2 July 1934, at least eighty-three men had lost their lives.

The 'Night of the Long Knives' was an important watershed in Nazi politics for three reasons: hitherto Hitler had acted within a legal framework, but during the purge he became overnight a totalitarian dictator. In providing the execution squads and firing parties the SS had taken the first criminal step along the road to eternal damnation, and finally on 20 July 1934 Hitler decreed 'In view of the great services rendered by the SS, particularly in connection with the events of 30 June 1934, I hereby promote the SS to the status of independent formation of the NSDAP.'

Now Himmler could embark on a process of consolidation while Heydrich set about unifying the secret police forces into one all-powerful SS secret service. This was no easy matter because not only did Heydrich have to overcome the reluctance of the civil authorities to surrender control over secret police activities, but also anti-SS feeling amongst the professional secret police officials. Himmler was obliged to make a number of tactical concessions but these were rendered meaningless when in June 1936 his party post of *Reichsführer-SS* was amalgamated with a newly created ministerial appointment of Chief of the German Police in the Reich Ministry of the Interior. This *Führer* decree went some way to overcoming the SS problem of lack of executive powers. As Reich Leader of the SS Himmler was virtually powerless, but as Chief of Police and later Minister of the Interior he acquired power over life and death.

Having overcome, bypassed or simply ignored the legislative barriers, Himmler and Heydrich were still confronted by personnel and sphere of activity problems. When the SS took over the Gestapo in April 1934, the SD became superfluous, but Himmler chose not to disband it because he wished to retain the SD's unique position as sole intelligence service of the Nazi Party. He also envisaged the SD and Gestapo as two intermeshing cogs in the same Reich security apparatus, but such an ideal state of affairs was never to be.

Many senior Gestapo officials expected no less than the sack when Heydrich took over the Gestapo, but the SD chief was sufficiently astute to see that even the most dedicated anti-Nazi police official could be seduced by the lure of unlimited police power and unlimited funds. Men with such names as Heinrich 'Gestapo' Müller, Josef Huber and Arthur Nebe soon became as ruthless as any Nazi in the service of absolute power. They paid lip-service to National Socialism, even donned SS uniform, but they resisted all SS attempts to replace the 'routine of the trained civil servant by revolutionary dynamism'.

In 1933 the SD had one hundred full-time staff and another hundred part-time helpers, who had hardly been involved in Hitler's seizure of power and despite their participation in the purge of the SA they felt eclipsed by the experienced professionals of the Gestapo. The type of young SD leader whom Heydrich was recruiting were mostly university graduates who had been trained for the legal profession. Their intellectual approach to the problem of ensuring complete loyalty to the Nazi regime resembled not so much a secret service, but a society of hyper-intelligent youth leaders:

'They were the flotsam from the wreckage left by the social disintegration which had overtaken the German middle class in the early 1930s; they were the rearguard of the bourgeoisie which had lost its faith in the pre-war standard of values. These young men born in the period 1900–1912, took their cue from the Völkisch★ wing of the German Youth Movement. They had matured in an atmosphere of disgust with the tottering democracy of Weimar and believed that in place of the "decadent" republic a better, specifically German, regime must be installed, superior to its Western counterparts.'

They were bound by three factors:

'The disintegration of the bourgeoisie, the traumatic experience of Versailles, and the hallucination that only by the strictest discipline and self-sacrifice could the Fatherland once again be raised to its former position of greatness. Patriotic speeches by their professors reinforced the youngsters' blind devotion to their country. Many of them were law students and the doctrine then holding sway in the legal faculties of the German universities placed State power high in the scheme of values.'

Since the SD and Gestapo were duplicating each others' efforts and chasing the same enemies, Heydrich tried in July 1937 to resolve the problem by allotting Marxism, treason and emigrés to the Gestapo. The SD was given the very wide field of ideological research which included science, Germanism, folklore, art, education, party and State, constitution and administration, freemasonry and miscellaneous societies. This did not please the SD who pointed out that as a party organization the SD had pride of place. The Gestapo had only come into being to meet a legal and administrative requirement of the State. What the Third Reich needed was a more 'potent guarantee of the State's security, springing from and vitalized by the will of a political movement'.

One very important area of activity not covered by this

★A general term for the various post-World War political groupings of ultra-nationalist and socialist parties with folk and racialist overtones.

agreement was foreign intelligence. The SD often found itself pursuing its enemies into neighbouring countries, and began to mount killing and intelligence-gathering operations outside Germany. The SD had no experience of foreign espionage, and so it was not long before it began to tread on the toes of Germany's military intelligence service or *Abwehr* which was run by Heydrich's old acquaintance Admiral Canaris. On 21 December 1936 Heydrich and Canaris drew up the 'ten commandments' which laid down spheres of activity for the *Abwehr* and Gestapo. The *Abwehr* would deal with espionage abroad and counter-intelligence at home. The Gestapo would deal with treason inside Germany.

On his appointment as *Reichsführer-SS* and Chief of the German police in June 1936 he could begin the process of uniting the SS and police into what he liked to call the State Protection Corps. But the SS was still struggling with a number of fundamental organizational and personnel problems which had to be overcome if the security services of the Reich, with their different backgrounds, practices and authorities, were to be welded into one all-powerful Nazi security service.

The original SD regional organization was based not on the military districts (*Wehrkreisen*) like the *Allgemeine-SS*, but on the *Länder*. The seven SD regions (*SD-Oberabschnitte*) which after September 1939 were known as (*SD-Leitabschnitte*) each controlled two or three sub-districts (*SD-Abschnitte*). The sub-districts were made up of a number of out-stations (*SD-Aussenstelle*) which covered the parishes. The field-workers were the *V-Männer* or informers. In 1937 there were some 50,000 unpaid informers most of whom were unaware that they were in fact working for the SD.

Parallel to this SD network, there were the Criminal Police offices, State Police (Gestapo) offices, and the Gestapo frontier stations which controlled the people leaving and entering Germany.

In an effort to co-ordinate the activities of the Gestapo and Criminal Police Heydrich created the post of Inspector of

Security Police (IdS) in September 1936. Then on 13 November 1937 he appointed the SS regional commanders Senior SS and Police Leaders or (*Höhere-SS-und-Polizeiführer*) with authority over all SS and police units in their region. These two powerful appointments conflicted with many of the duties traditionally carried out by the Police President, and it was not until the appointment of a Senior SS and Police Commander in each of the occupied territories that the system worked effectively.

Himmler's plans to unify the SS and police began to threaten the very existence of the SD. As more and more Gestapo officials joined the SD, the old SD men saw themselves being swamped by rank-parity Gestapo officials who were often not even members of the NSDAP or SS. In mid-1936 only 244 out of the 607 Gestapo officials belonged to the SS, and when, at the outbreak of war, the Gestapo had grown to 20,000, only 3,000 were SS members. Another cause of resentment was the shortage of funds in the SD compared with the Gestapo, nor did SD men enjoy the same pension rights as their colleagues from the civil service.

Heydrich decided that the SD and Security Police must merge officially so that the SD could also become a State organization paid for by the Reich. When on 27 September 1939 the Reich Security Main Office came into existence it was for internal administrative convenience only, and the union was kept semi-secret. Despite the merging of its departments and personnel, party and State refused to mix, and the sinister schism continued until the end of the Third Reich.

Concentration Camps
1933-1945

*Above all personal feelings and considerations
and above all selfishness stands the iron law to
which we everywhere must always remain true.*

THEODOR EICKE

Concentration camps came into existence in Germany in 1933 as a direct result of Hitler's determination, as newly elected Chancellor, to eliminate all political opposition and restore Germany to the rule of law. The emergency decree for the Protection of the People and State which came into force on 28 February 1933, empowered the authorities to detain, for up to three months, anyone considered to be a threat to the newly established government. When the state of emergency was over this ordinance had outlived its original purpose, but it was never rescinded. The concept of 'protective custody' which was embodied in this ordinance enabled the Nazis to create and maintain a police state until the end of their existence.

The police of the Weimar Republic was the executive instrument of an authoritarian and patriarchal society, but it acted strictly within the law. Most policemen had at one time or another served in the armed forces, and tended to sympathize more with the ultra-nationalist Nazis than the internationalists of the Communist Party, but to their credit they had acted with equal vigour against all radicals, and there was little love lost between the Brownshirts and the police.

Hermann Göring, as Minister President of Prussia, ordered

the police, assisted by 15,000 SA and SS men who had been sworn in as auxiliary policemen, to round up all political opponents. Personal vendetta and denunciation swelled the numbers detained to such an extent that prisons were soon filled to overflowing. Many were released soon after, but in July 1933 there were still 26,789 'opponents' held in protective custody throughout the Reich. Disused factories were taken over as makeshift detention centres and run by the police, but guarded by auxiliaries from the SA and SS. Conditions in these semi-derelict and draughty factories were primitive in the extreme, beds and bedding were often non-existent, while cooking and sanitary facilities were sparse. The treatment of prisoners tended to vary. In those camps formed as annexes of conventional prisons and run by the police, treatment was harsh but not vindictive. But there was another type of illegal camp which was run by the local SA, and in these so-called 'wild' camps sadistic brutality was the rule rather than the exception.

Like many ordinary Germans, Wolf Sendele knew about the existence of these early camps:

'We knew well enough that these camps existed, detention camps, or whatever they were called, and that political opponents were being incarcerated. We were never quite clear why. God knows, the crimes themselves were not serious enough to remove a man from his house and home. But you thought to yourself – it's just a temporary measure, they'll put them away in a camp for three or four weeks, and then let them go again, when they've established that they're just harmless fellows – not like Thälmann [leader of the German Communist Party – KPD] or people who were real agitators.'

As the months passed and calm returned, there was an increasing outcry against the continued detention of innocent people in concentration camps. To make matters worse for the Nazi Party the relatives of men who had disappeared under suspicious circumstances in the 'wild' camps were instituting legal proceedings, and there was a Ministry of Justice and a number of lawyers who still believed in the rule of law and in justice. The stories of the most terrible excesses which prevailed in the concentration camps also began to hit the headlines in foreign newspapers and the Nazi Party, which was still trying to maintain the façade of a constitutional government, refuted all charges and even published detailed rebuttals. Before being released prisoners were forced to sign a paper stating that they had been well treated during protective custody, and they were warned that if they ever spoke about their treatment to the press, either in Germany or abroad, their relatives would suffer the consequences.

In March 1933 a cluster of old brick factory buildings at Dachau, near Munich, was hurriedly prepared by a detachment from the Volunteer Labour Service, and on 20 March detainees from the various small camps and prisons in Bavaria began to be concentrated in Dachau. This new camp with a planned capacity of 5,000 prisoners was the responsibility of Heinrich Himmler in his capacity as Commander of the Bavarian Political Police.

The SS guard unit at Dachau was drawn from the 56th SS Foot Regiment which had already acquired an unsavoury reputation even in SS circles. *SS-Oberführer* (brigadier) Hildebrandt was Leader of SS District South and his staff used Dachau as a dump for all its unwanted men. The first commandant was *SS-Sturmhauptführer* (captain) Hilmar Wäckerle and he set about drafting draconian regulations, and instituting a system of classification of the inmates, but he did nothing to improve the discipline or morale of his guard detachment, so that maltreatment became so widespread and uncontrolled that eventually Wäckerle, the camp doctor and the Gestapo official were charged by the Public Prosecutor's office in Munich with aiding and abetting in the murder of a prisoner. Himmler had no choice but to sack Wäckerle.

The new commandant of Dachau was *SS-Oberführer* (brigadier) Theodor Eicke, a rough unstable character whose violent and unruly behaviour had already given Himmler many headaches. At last Himmler found an ideal backwater for his troublesome subordinate and sent him off to Dachau.

Eicke found that, 'There were times when we had no coats, no boots, no socks. Without so much as a murmur, our men wore their own clothes on duty. We were generally regarded as a necessary evil that only cost money; little men of no consequence standing guard behind barbed wire. The pay of my officers and men, meagre though it was, I had to beg from the various State Finance Offices. As *Oberführer* I earned in Dachau 230 *Reichmark* per month and was fortunate because I enjoyed the confidence of my *Reichsführer* [Himmler]. At the beginning there was not a single cartridge, not a single rifle, let alone machine guns. Only three of my men knew how to operate a machine gun. They slept in draughty factory halls. Everywhere there was poverty and want. At the time these men belonged to SS District South. They left it to me to take care of my men's troubles but, unasked, sent men they wanted to be rid of in Munich for some reason or another. These misfits polluted my unit and troubled its state of mind. I had to contend with disloyalty, embezzlement and corruption. Matters did not progress because my men were under orders of District South and were used as a backwater for so-called "superannuation candidates". When I saw that things did not improve, the *Reichsführer* acceded to my request, and placed the small guard unit entirely under my own command.

'From now on progress was unimpeded. I set to work unreservedly and joyfully; I trained soldiers as non-commissioned officers, and non-commissioned officers as leaders. United in our readiness for sacrifice and suffering and in cordial comradeship we created in a few weeks an excellent discipline which produced an outstanding *esprit de corps*. We did not become megalomaniacs, because we were all poor. Behind the barbed-wire fence we quietly did our duty, and without pity cast out from our ranks anyone who showed the least sign of disloyalty. Thus moulded and thus trained, the camp guard unit grew in the quietness of the concentration camp. Its ideals were "loyalty, bravery and devotion to duty".'

Eicke's re-organization of Dachau created the model for all future SS concentration camps. He drafted a new disciplinary code for inmates, and formalized the division of responsibility between the concentration camp staff and the guard unit. He forbade arbitrary maltreatment of inmates by guards, not out of any humanitarian feelings, but because it was bad for discipline, and because the SS had to be careful not to become involved in any scandals, such as those which had taken place in the summer of 1933. Instead he introduced varying degrees of punishment ranging from withdrawal of privileges to solitary confinement and corporal punishment. In extreme cases the commandant had the power to sentence an inmate to death and carry out the sentence within the confines of the camp without reference to any judicial authority.

The ritualized beating of prisoners was intended not only to humiliate and punish the offender but to deter other inmates, and at the same time to harden the guards. Rudolf Höss, who was later commandant of Auschwitz, served his apprenticeship in the Dachau guard unit:

'I can clearly remember the first flogging that I witnessed. Eicke had issued orders that a minimum of one company from the guard unit must attend the infliction of these corporal punishments.

'Two prisoners who had stolen cigarettes from the canteen were sentenced to twenty-five lashes each with the whip.

'The troops under arms were formed up in an open square in the centre of which stood the whipping block (*Bock*).

'Two prisoners were led forward by their block leaders. Then the commandant arrived. The commander of the protective custody compound and the senior company commander reported to him.

'The *Rapportführer* read out the sentence and the first prisoner, a small impenitent malingerer, was made to lie along the length of the *Bock*. Two soldiers held his head and hands and two block leaders carried out the punishment, delivering alternate strokes. The prisoner uttered no sound. The other prisoner, a professional politician of strong physique, behaved quite differently. He cried out at the very first stroke and tried to break free. He went on screaming to the end, although the commandant yelled at him to keep quiet. I was standing in the first rank and was compelled to watch the whole procedure. I say compelled, because if I had been in the rear I would not have looked. When the man began to scream I went hot and cold all over. In fact the whole thing, even the beating of the first prisoner made me shudder. Later on, at the beginning of the war, I attended my first execution, but it did not affect me nearly so much as witnessing that first corporal punishment.'

Höss was quite typical of Eicke's raw material. The average youth who volunteered for service with the Dachau guard unit often came from the countryside, either to escape from a stifling home life, or in the search for adventure. Eicke realized that such men had to be trained to hate, and he systematically broke down any sympathy that his men might feel towards the prisoner by continuously portraying them as vermin, sub-humans and as dangerous criminals. SS men were warned never to drop their guard for one instant, or they might fall victim to those whom Hitler in his wisdom had put behind barbed wire.

Herman Langbein who spent four years in concentration camps remembers a young SS man, Hans Stark, who hung a sign above his desk in Auschwitz, on which was written in Gothic script 'Sympathy is Weakness' (*Mitleid ist Schwache*), and Langbein maintains that it was this philosophy which was drummed into young SS men, that enabled them to tolerate and even take part in dreadful atrocities, without feeling any sense of guilt.

As the SS took over the running of all concentration camps many of the makeshift 'wild' camps were closed down and the inmates either were released or concentrated in seven main camps – Dachau, Esterwegen, Lichtenburg, Sachsenburg, Oranienburg, Columbia House and Fuhlsbüttel. The process of reducing the number of camps and building vast new complexes continued until in 1938 there were four main camps guarded by four regiments of Death's Head Guards which on formation in July 1937 had a strength of 4,449 officers and men.

The four main camps (*Hauptlager*) were each comprised of three main parts. The original camp became the protective custody compound in which the inmates lived in huts, and included the *Kommandantur* or commandant's office. Around the protective custody compound sprang up an SS camp which in Dachau was known as the training camp (*Übungslager*). This included quarters for the camp staff and barracks for the guard unit, workshops and stores. The third part was known as the *Wirtschaftsbetriebe* or industrial works where the camp inmates were employed in making clothing for the inmates, uniforms for the SS, and furniture and other fittings for the SS barracks and headquarters.

The orderly running of the huts or blocks, and discipline amongst the inmates, was the responsibility of the inmate hierarchy appointed by the SS from amongst the German criminals. In each compound there was a Camp Senior who was in charge of the various ranks of Capo. These men usually wore the green triangle of the German criminal and were known in camp jargon as 'greens'. Some Capos curried favour with the 'SS-lers' by behaving with exaggerated brutality towards their fellow inmates, but there was also another class of inmate which was used by the SS in the smooth running of a concentration camp. These men were the German-speaking political prisoners who wore the red triangle. They were employed as clerks and hospital orderlies, and in these positions some of them tried in various subtle ways to alleviate the sufferings of their less-fortunate comrades. With the establishment of concentration camps in Poland, German politicals were transferred to the new camps where they would constitute a trusted group which was given minor privileges, but considerable responsibility by the SS.

Like Höss many of the young men who answered Himmler's

call to join the ranks of the full-time SS as members of a unit guarding a concentration camp were peasants or artisans from the rural areas. In their rustic seclusion they didn't really know what concentration camps were. On arrival the young recruit would be subjected to the worst kind of Prussian martinetry. One former concentration camp inmate remembers that the sight of an SS sergeant kicking a new recruit didn't give him any pleasure, because he thought 'if they treat each other like that what can we expect?' Pressure was put on the SS men to renounce their faith, and by 1938 69 per cent of the *SS-Totenkopfverbände* had left the church. The SS man was continuously harangued about the enemies of the state and how dangerous they were, and then he was marched into the protective custody compound to witness a flogging. And yet in this harsh, cruel and humourless world Eicke still succeeded in not only winning the popularity of his men, who called him 'Papa' Eicke, but forging a body of men who would carry out any order, however inhuman, which their *Reichsführer* might give them without so much as a murmur.

Young men volunteered for service in the SS-TV for either four or twelve years, while officers had to sign on for twenty-five years. Since service in the SS-TV did not count as national service the twenty-one-year-old SS man had to do his military service in either the armed SS (*SS-Verfügungstruppe*) or the *Wehrmacht*. On completion of his military service he might return to the SS-TV, he might find the excitement and glamour of the military life more attractive than the stillness and monotony of the concentration camp. Eicke would continuously drum into his men that 'we belong neither to the Army nor the Police, nor the SS-VT; our cohesion is based upon the comradeship inherent in our National Socialist identity'.

As far as officers were concerned service in the SS Death's Head unit was not necessarily voluntary. Himmler was anxious to create a new breed of young SS leader with all-round experience of SS work. On graduating from one of the

1. Gauleiter Dr Josef Goebbels addresses a political meeting in Berlin in 1932. An SS man stands guard between the speaker and his audience.

2. An *Einsatzgruppen*
execution in Russia
watched by German
military personnel, 1942.

3. *Allgemeine-SS* men on
street-lining duty during
a visit by the Führer,
May 1936.

4. Hitler addresses the Reichstag. On his right his personal adjutant Julius Schaub, and on the left *Waffen-SS* adjutant Richard Schulze, 1940.

5. Weary *Waffen-SS* grenadiers on the eastern front, February 1944.

6. Richard Schulze in the uniform of a captain in the *Leibstandarte-SS Adolf Hitler*.

7. Richard Schulze-Kossens being interviewed by Thames Television in Düsseldorf in May 1980.

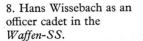

8. Hans Wissebach as an officer cadet in the *Waffen-SS*.

9. Hans Wissebach photographed in his office in the 'Lange Eugen' in Bonn, May 1980.

10. Reichsführer-SS Heinrich Himmler and Chief of Staff of the SA Ernst Röhm at an SS rally, August 1933.

11. Goebbels with Hitler's chauffeur Julius Schreck (on right). On left Emil Maurice one of the first SS men and faithful follower of his Führer, until his Jewish background was discovered.

12. SA and SS men about to put the torch to Communist banners, 1933.

13. The SS ideal; a blond SS man with his 'handsome' wife and blond children.

THE HOHENHORST BASTARDS OF HIMMLER'S MEN ARE BLUE-EYED, FLAXEN-HAIRED AND PIG-FAT. THEY MUST EAT PORRIDGE WHETHER THEY WANT TO OR

"SUPER BABIES"

Illegitimate children of SS men are housed in a German chateau

Last fortnight LIFE Photographer Robert Capa visited a German chateau which housed a Nazi establishment known as a *Lebensborn*, or "Well-of-Life," home. At the Hohenhorst *Lebensborn* home, as in many such institutions in Germany, live dozens of illegitimate babies who have no father or mother but the now-defunct Nazi state. They are the products of an official government policy of encouraging illegitimacy to keep up the country's birth rate. Soldiers going off to war were urged to do their bit, whether married or not. The government promised to care for illegitimate offspring, to honor and respect unwed mothers.

The Nazi bastards at Hohenhorst, aged 2 to 5, are children of SS men encouraged by Heinrich Himmler to father "super babies." Grown pig-fat under care and overstuffing of Nazi nurses, they now pose for the Allies a problem yet to be solved.

14. A page from *Life Magazine* showing the types of Aryan babies found by American occupation forces in a 'Lebensborn' home at Hohenhorst. (Time/Life)

two SS Cadet Schools, a subaltern would serve a tour of duty with each branch of the SS. The output of the SS Cadet Schools was far too large to be absorbed by the *SS-Verfügungstruppe* and so many young officers found there were no vacancies in the regiment of their choice. Instead they had to serve in one of the Death's Head units or the police. Once in a regiment, he was also expected to serve on detachment to the SD or one of the other branches of the SS, or he might be transferred to a Death's Head Regiment, and this became more common in the years 1939 and 1940 when the armed SS was being rapidly expanded.

The size of the commandant's staff varied from camp to camp and from time to time, but it usually numbered between 200 and 250 men. Most of them were employed in the *Kommandantur* and in the running of the camp hospital (revier), stores, kitchens, workshops and garages, while the rest were responsible for controlling the inmates. Their titles are engraved on the memories of those inmates who survived, because it was these officials who imposed the regime under which all the inmates lived. Most of these men carried out their boring and monotonous jobs in accordance with the regulations – neither doing more nor less than was expected of them, but there were also those who enlivened their tedious duties by practising every kind of chicanery on their charges with every degree of physical and mental cruelty which often bordered on the sadistic.

The commandant's most important subordinates were the adjutant, who was responsible for the day to day running of the camp as a whole, and the protective custody commander (*Schutzhaftlagerführer*) whose office was in the gatehouse (*Jourhaus*) through which everyone had to enter or leave the compound. He shared the building with the Gestapo official who kept the prisoners' records, and also acted as a representative of Reinhard Heydrich's Security Police headquarters and liaised with the local Police authorities.

Other SS camp staff who were allowed to enter the compound and who had dealings with the inmates were mostly hard-bitten SS non-commissioned officers with little or no military experience nor decorations. The most senior was the Roll Call Leader (*Rapportführer*) who was responsible for conducting the roll calls which Hermann Langbein remembers so well:

'We had to march out at dawn onto the parade ground for early morning roll call. It was always a dreadful military ceremony. Everyone had to stand bolt upright in rows. The order "hats off" had to be done with total precision. If there was some mistake or other, then there were punishment exercises. Then the SS took the roll call – to check whether the numbers tallied. That was always the most important thing in every concentration camp – the numbers *had* to be right at every roll call. No one was allowed to be absent. It made no difference if someone had died during the night – the body would be laid out and included in the roll. And then, when roll call was over, we had to form up into our working parties. And every working party had its own assembly area, which one had to know in order to line up. And then the parties set off for work – depending on whether one was working inside the camp or outside. The outside parties were escorted by SS men. The working day was determined by the time of year. Work was determined by hours of daylight, not the clock. The parties could only leave camp when it was already half-light, so that people couldn't escape under cover of darkness. Work lasted 'till noon. At midday we formed up and ate lunch. There were some working parties who had their food outside the camp. It was a kind of soup, that had a few bits and pieces floating about; it was difficult to identify what exactly. And then we carried on working until the evening roll call. In the evening, the working parties formed up again on the parade ground. The same military ceremony, which is described here much faster than the time it actually took. We were counted up again, and if the figures were correct, if the roll call was in order, we were allowed to march off into the blocks – to our own living quarters – and we had to sing as we went; and woe betide anyone who didn't sing. We were so

40

sick of the songs – "The Hazelnut is Black and Brown" is one I recall very well.'

As long as German concentration camps continued to be a political extension of the German prison system, pre-war conditions and routine were maintained, but following the German invasion of the Soviet Union in June 1941 camps became increasingly crowded and conditions deteriorated rapidly. The camp population on 15 January 1945 was 714,211 of whom 202,674 were women. During the war not only the purpose of the camps underwent a change, but many new categories of prisoner found themselves in concentration camps. To those imprisoned for political or racial crimes, and criminals, were added nationalists, patriots, spies and resistance workers from the occupied territories, and certain categories of prisoners of war who were not protected by the Geneva Convention, mainly from the Red Army.

This incredible conglomeration of nations, races and religions suffered in a brutal and dangerous environment, under the constant threat of death and physical violence, cut off from all news of their loved ones, and finally became a pawn in the constant struggle for power within the Nazi hierarchy.

Those Nazis, who believed fanatically in the racial myth or who stood to enrich themselves at the expense of their victims, were happy to exterminate every 'sub-human' they could lay their hands on, but there was another more intelligent – but equally cruel – group which believed that Germany should first win the war before beginning the biological struggle.

Concentration camp labour became increasingly important to the German war effort as more and more German industrial workers were called up for service in the armed forces. Many of those killed by the Security Police in the occupied Eastern territories were often artisans, and sometimes highly trained technicians, whose skills could have been utilized prior to extermination. This conflict of interests – in which human compassion and morality played no part – was reflected in the wartime development of the German concentration camps.

In October 1939, Theodor Eicke was appointed commander of an SS division, and his place as Inspector of Concentration Camps was taken over by Richard Glücks. For ten months the Inspectorate came under the SS Main Office (*SS-Hauptamt*) but in August 1940 a new operational headquarters for the Waffen-SS was formed under *SS-Brigadeführer* (brigadier-general) Hans Jüttner to command the Waffen-SS, but nobody was quite sure which parts of the SS organization formed part of the Waffen-SS. On the 22 April 1941 the *SS-Führungshauptamt* issued a directive which listed one hundred and sixty-three units, departments and installations considered to be part of the Waffen-SS. This list included the staffs and guard units of the eight main concentration camps. So for nearly a year the concentration camps came under control of Hans Jüttner and the operational headquarters of the Waffen-SS. The most notable manifestation of this decree was that concentration camp guards became members of the Waffen-SS with the same uniform and badges of rank and carried Waffen-SS pay-books. It meant also that members of a concentration camp staff or guard unit could be transferred to another Waffen-SS unit at the front, or a Waffen-SS man serving in one of the field formations could be sent to join the staff of a concentration camp on grounds of ill-health or physical disability which rendered him unfit for front line duty.

This was the most cogent argument against those SS apologists who claim that the Waffen-SS had nothing to do with the concentration camps. On both the highest formal and lowest guard level Himmler had irrevocably bound the knights of his black order to the murkiest corners of his deadly empire.

The final transfer of control over the concentration camps came in February 1942, when the Inspectorate of Concentration Camps became Section D (*Amtsgruppe D*) of Oswald Pohl's SS Economic and Administrative Main Office (*SS-*

Wirtschafts-Verwaltungs Hauptamt, or WHVA for short). Pohl was a former naval paymaster and one of those SS pragmatists with considerable business acumen, organizational ability and complete lack of scruples. As soon as Pohl's office became the largest employer of concentration camp labour, it fell foul of the 'final solution fanatics' in Reinhard Heydrich's Reich Security Main Office or RSHA.

Pohl insisted on better treatment for camp inmates, and SS men were forbidden to strike, kick or even touch a prisoner. Inmates were to be better housed and fed, and even encouraged to take an interest in their work. Those who did were to be trained and rewarded with their freedom. There was a small reduction in the number of cases of maltreatment, but food and accommodation were still appalling, and in return for these 'improvements' prisoners were still expected to work eleven hours per day, six or seven days a week.

After the initial wave of pogrom-like massacres, the SS and police gathered the surviving Jews of occupied Poland and the Ukraine in ghettoes and labour camps. The SS supplied the raw materials and tools – much of which had been stolen from Jewish firms – and Jewish sweated labour manufactured goods for the SS.

These makeshift industries had enabled many Jews to survive, and the output of these factories was considered by SS procurement offices to be of great value, but around these activities a vast web of SS corruption grew up.

In an attempt to regularize the situation, which was rapidly getting out of hand, Oswald Pohl formed a limited company called Eastern Industries or *Osti* to manage the ghetto and labour camp work shops. 'The very word *Osti* makes me sick' was the typical reaction of the exterminators, and as soon as possible Reinhard Heydrich sabotaged the enterprise by summoning the *Osti* Jews to the gas chambers in November 1943. In the view of the RSHA, according to Rudolf Höss, 'every new labour camp and every additional thousand workers increased the risk that one day they might be set free or somehow continue to remain alive'. If today you speak to a Jewish survivor of the holocaust, he usually owes his survival to the fact that he was employed in an SS industry.

The SS 1933-1939

SS man! Your honour is loyalty

ADOLF HITLER

On 30 January 1933 Hitler became Chancellor of the German Reich and his jubilant followers waited in impatient expectation for their just rewards. SA leaders and men hoped above all for regular employment. SS men expected to be made senior police officials, while their leaders aspired to nothing less than the Police Presidency. *Gauleiters* of the Nazi Party saw themselves as State Presidents or at least Aldermen (*Stadtrat*). Wolf Sendale remembers that 'It should have been a day of unbelievable celebration, a day of rejoicing because we'd done it at last. Hitler is going to be Chancellor and we've won the Party battle.' But Hitler's election soon gave way to misgivings. 'The fighting side of things – if we can call it that – was pushed into the background. There were no more marches and propaganda wasn't needed any more because Hitler had been elected. The young men, young SS men, Hitler Youth, the young National Socialists were affected because the element of struggle had just disappeared, and those people that we had respected earlier because they had really thrown themselves into the struggle, were now only worried about getting a seat in Parliament or becoming a *Gauleiter* or some other sinecure which was more or less a life insurance policy.'

Now that Hitler was in power there was a veritable stream of applicants to join the Nazi Party, many of whom had purely opportunistic reasons. The SS with its smart new black uniforms attracted more and more barons and counts, and these aristocrats had a considerable influence on the direction of the SS command in Berlin.

Not only the personnel, but also the organizational direction of the SS began to change in 1933 as Himmler worked insidiously to establish his own power base. The SS began to split up into three distinct branches each with its own clearly defined role. The first was the *Sicherheitsdienst* or SD which had been formed by Reinhard Heydrich in early 1931, as a direct result of the feuds which had wracked the NSDAP in that year and in the years that followed. The next branch was the SS Political Readiness Squads (*SS-Politische Bereitschaften*). These company-sized armed units were the forerunners of the *Waffen-SS*. Some of these detachments had been formed to guard the newly-established SS concentration camps and they later became the SS Death's Head Formations (*SS-Totenkopfverbände*). From mid-1934 that part of the SS which did not belong to any of these special branches was called the *Allgemeine* or General SS. At first the distinction between the branches was blurred, but gradually Himmler imposed his centralized command over the independently minded old guard of SS regional commanders, so that each of these branches soon had its own chain of command.

1933 and 1934 were critical years for the SS. Although it had been tacitly agreed that the SS should never exceed 10 per cent of the strength of the SA, the 52,000-strong SS deliberately opened its doors to all comers and began a period of rapid expansion.

At the beginning of 1934 Hitler was still trying to restore normality in his nervous Reich, but in so doing he increasingly antagonized the radical wing of his party. The SA, whose four million members were still clamouring for more sweeping reforms and a larger slice of the cake, was becoming an embarrassment to Hitler. During the *Kampfzeit* the

46

hard-drinking, hard-swearing and hard-hitting, ex-soldiers who typified the bulk of the SA leadership had by sheer ruthlessness struck terror into the hearts of Hitler's opponents and literally driven them off the streets. But in the post-revolutionary phase Hitler was looking for a different type of man and those who now joined the party were careerists and professional men who had been schooled in Weimarian Germany, but had not been tainted by democratic scruples.

In a deft move Hitler, aided by the SS and with the approval of the *Reichswehr*, purged the SA of its most radical and independently minded leaders. The purge of the SA freed the SS from subordination to the SA, and on 20 July 1934 the SS was proclaimed an independent formation of the NSDAP. In carrying out the execution of sixteen SA leaders and many other opponents of Nazism, the SS succeeded in earning the undying hatred of the SA rank-and-file, and the fear of all moderate Germans. As the shots from the SS firing squads shattered the stillness of the summer night in Berlin Lichterfelde, they heralded the end of the rule of law and the beginning of eleven terrible years for the SS, its victims and the German people.

Now that Himmler was leader of his own independent SS, he could embark on his dream of creating an elite order of magnificent Germanic manhood. While the *Reichsführer* became more and more preoccupied with the minutiae of his fantastic vision, subordinates like Karl Wolff paid lip-service to their chief, while finding his ideas slightly ridiculous. Sadly for them they didn't realize until it was too late (if at all) that in the SS Himmler had the means to make a reality of his perverted ideas on race and breeding.

In 1933 and 1934 the SS increased its membership from 50,000 to 400,000 through widespread and indiscriminate recruitment – even some Jews succeeded in joining the SS. Since the foundation of the Hitler Youth movement in 1926 many volunteers came to the SS from the Hitler Youth. During the period of the struggle when service in the Hitler Youth was still voluntary (it became compulsory in

December 1936) a special relationship developed between the youth and the SS.

'The HJ – as we called them – were just kids who we used to take under our wing and protect when they went on marches, because it was great fun for the Communists to push the youths about and bash them up, so we used to protect them. There was always excellent understanding between us and the HJ, so they became our cadets so to speak, and we knew that one day they would join our ranks.'

People came to the SS in many different ways. There were some, like Karl Wolff, who applied to join one of the other formations of the Nazi Party, but was persuaded to join the SS. There were others who simply applied to join at an SS office. The Nazi Party was very keen on sport and sporting events provided a good opportunity to propagandize on behalf of the party. Socially sport was a very good leveller and it was another professed aim of National Socialism to create a classless society in Germany. Athletic youths made good soldiers and so it became obligatory for all undergraduates to complete at least two athletic courses before graduation. Dr Konrad Morgen, who later became an SS judge, found it a sensible and healthy idea because German students spent all their time cooped up in their studies or drinking beer. In 1932 Morgen attended the College of Physical Training in Frankfurt and underwent a course of light athletics. In 1933 SA and SS leaders began to appear on the sports field and it was not long before a makeshift uniform was introduced for the participants. Then the sports themselves began to take on a more military flavour. Finally the course was divided into two groups and Dr Morgen's was told to join the SS.

Hans Wissebach, now a Conservative member of the Federal German Parliament, remembers that it was a sports rally in Nuremburg in 1937 that he saw SS troops for the first time. He and his colleagues were so impressed that they all wanted to join up, but out of eighty applicants only ten were accepted.

Richard Böck was a musician when it was suggested that the

whole band in which he played should transfer to the SS, but unfortunately not all the bandsmen were tall enough for service in the Foot Regiments, so they became a cavalry band. Böck and some of the bandsmen were not happy about being transferred, but they had all put so much into the band, and Böck felt he couldn't swim against the tide. That decision, taken in the early 1930s at a time when it would have been very easy to opt out, was to lead him to Auschwitz where he served as a guard.

Himmler realized that the mass recruitment which had taken place in 1933 was very damaging to the elite status of the SS and so in 1934 and 1935 200,000 SS men were discharged on moral, racial and physical grounds. In order to control the new intake of recruits and to enhance the concept of the SS as an Order, Himmler borrowed freely from the Jesuit Order and introduced a complex three year enrolment procedure.

Having been declared physically and racially suitable for SS membership, an eighteen-year-old youth became an Applicant (*Bewerber*). In September of that year, during the annual Reich Party Day Rally in Nuremburg, he became a Candidate (*Anwärter*) and received an SS identity card and an SS number. As a Candidate he was expected to win both the SA Military and Reich Sports Badges during his first year of service. At the end of this probationary period he swore the oath of allegiance to Adolf Hitler on 9 November, at a torchlit ceremony in the Odeonsplatz in Munich facing the Feldherrnhalle monument.

> I swear to thee Adolf Hitler
> As Führer and Chancellor of the
> German Reich
> Loyalty and bravery
> I vow to thee and the superiors
> Whom thou shalt appoint
> Obedience unto death
> So help me God.

Next he would be called up for his obligatory six months' service in the Reich Labour Corps, after which he would return once more to his SS unit. At twenty-one he became liable for military service which lasted two years. On return to civilian life and his SS unit, and having satisfied all SS requirements and thoroughly familiarized himself with the SS marriage code and code of honour, the SS Candidate would become a full SS man on the following 9 November. All members of the SS regardless of rank were first and foremost an *SS-Mann*.

On 9 November he was also given the right to wear the SS dagger, and at the presentation ceremony vowed that he and his relations would for ever observe the fundamental laws of the SS. From that day on it was his right and duty to defend his honour according to the Code of Honour of the Black Corps.

As an SS man he would serve in SS1 until he was twenty-five, then SS2 until thirty-five, when he became a member of the SS Reserve. At forty-five he passed into the *SS-Stamm-abteilung*, which was a sort of supplementary reserve for founder members. It had been formed so that SS who were still fit could continue to serve the SS in a number of subtle but very important ways. Despite their age the stalwarts of the *Stammabteilung* were meshed into the intricate machinery of SS surveillance and control of the civilian population.

In the years leading up to World War II the typical part-time member of the *Allgemeine-SS* gave up one evening a week for ideological work and training. One afternoon, usually Wednesday or Saturday, was set aside for physical training and sport. One weekend in each month an SS man had to spend Saturday afternoon and Sunday on military training, important elements of which were drill, crowd control and shooting. The other three Sundays in the month were free.

This smart well-drilled and disciplined para-military force had an excellent *esprit de corps* which enabled the Nazi Party to maintain a large auxiliary police force at nominal cost. The

SS could be called out at short notice in case of a national emergency such as an anti-Nazi putsch, a rebellion, strike or some other civil disorder. In addition to their regular activities SS men took part in local ceremonies on national holidays and festivals. SS units participated in parades, processions, and wreath layings, and in September each year they sent a contingent complete with regimental standard to the greatest festival in the Nazi calendar – the annual Reich Party Day Rally in Nuremburg.

When SS men were needed to help the police with crowd control and security arrangements for a visit by Hitler or any other prominent member of the Nazi Party or foreign dignatory, SS headquarters in Berlin would summon SS men to duty with a printed postcard. An SS man's employer was forbidden by law to prevent or hinder his employee from responding to such a summons.

The last full year of peace was the thirteenth year of the existence of the SS. It now numbered 239,000 men, of which 8,995 were employed full-time in SS headquarters. Germany, now incorporating Austria into what was known as the Greater German Reich was divided into fourteen SS districts, thirty-eight sub-districts and one-hundred-and-four foot and nineteen cavalry regiments. In addition there were forty-two special motor transport, signals and engineer battalions, as well as a number of frontier guard units. To provide trained personnel for all these departments and units the SS established a number of schools and training establishments for administration, horsemanship, driving and physical training. In September 1937 a new school was opened at the SS complex at Dachau outside Munich for the training of junior leaders of the *Allgemeine-SS*.

Having described the pre-war organization and activities of the *Allgemeine-SS*, it must be remembered that members of the *Allgemeine-SS* were, unless acting under the authority of an officer of the State, civilians with no more or less rights than any other citizen. They were unarmed and subject to civil law and call-up in the armed forces. Not only were they expected to abide by the law, but Himmler in his school-masterish manner expected SS men to set an example to other Germans. SS men were not allowed to smoke or dance in public in uniform, nor could they go to proscribed clubs, beer cellars, or bars in which decadent 'nigger' jazz music was played. But probably the most unpopular and widely abused restriction on an SS man's personal freedom was the marriage order. From 31 December 1931 all marriages of SS men had to be approved by the SS Race Office or Himmler himself, and permission would be given 'only if the necessary conditions of race and healthy stock were fulfilled'.

The Armed SS 1933–1939

*The task of the SS is to guarantee the security
of Germany from the interior, just as the
Wehrmacht guarantees the integrity of the
honour, the greatness and the peace of the
Reich from the exterior.*

H. HIMMLER

In 1933 Himmler ordered SS regional leaders to form small
armed SS guard units, or special commandos (*Sonderkommandos*) to carry out special tasks of a political nature, which
may, from time to time, be assigned to him by the Führer.
These units were to grow in size and effectiveness until they
became, in 1940, the *Waffen-SS*.

For the first two years, Hitler's position as Reich Chancellor was by no means secure. He had to contend with the
suspicion and disapproval of the Reich government and its
executive arm – the 100,000-strong *Reichswehr* on the right,
and the growing dissatisfaction of the most radical wing of
his Party, the 4,000,000-strong SA, on the left. The only
section of the Nazi Party which had shown itself consistently
loyal and obedient was Himmler's SS, and so Hitler entrusted
one of his old bodyguards, Josef 'Sepp' Dietrich with the
formation of a small personal guard of *Stabswache* – the third
in the history of the SS – on 17 March 1933.

Sepp Dietrich was one of those quick-witted Bavarian
toughs who rode in Hitler's Mercedes during his speaking
tours, and whom the party wags dubbed the *chauffeureska*.

He was born into a peasant family at Hawangen in Bavaria
on 28 May 1892. After eight years of elementary school
(*Volksschule*) education he went to work in various European
hotels. During World War I he served in the Royal Bavarian
Army and ended the war as a highly decorated sergeant in

the 13th Bavarian Tank Battalion. After the war he served for a short time in the Bavarian Gendarmerie and then the *Bund Oberland Freikorps* which was one of the radical right-wing organizations which participated in the November 1923 Munich putsch.

Dietrich joined the SS in 1929 (SS No. 1177) while working as a shipper in the offices of the Nazi publisher Franz Eher, and soon became one of Hitler's constant companions. In the spring of 1931 he helped smash the Stennes Revolt and was rewarded with the rank of *SS-Gruppenführer* (lieutenant general) on 18 December 1931. In March 1933 he took command of the newly formed *SS-Stabswache* in Berlin, although he does not appear to have had much to do with this modest unit until it became the *Adolf Hitler Standarte* in September 1933. In October it was decided that this unit should be paid for not by the SS, but out of Reich funds, and this enabled Dietrich to distance the regiment from Himmler's control. Dietrich became a law unto himself, and even the formidable Inspector of the *SS-Verfügungstruppe* was only permitted to attend parades. Himmler was eventually able to re-establish his authority, although Dietrich, who always held military tradition in awe, had scant respect for the authority of the decidedly unmilitary Himmler.

As the only armed unit which was unquestionably loyal to Hitler, the *Leibstandarte SS Adolf Hitler* played a key role in the purge of the SA on 30 June 1934, and it was Dietrich's firing squads who carried out the summary executions in Berlin and Munich, and on 1 July 1934 Dietrich's reward was promotion to the rank of *SS-Obergruppenführer* (general).

In 1942 Hitler said that his former bodyguard was 'a man who is simultaneously cunning, energetic and brutal. Under his swashbuckling appearance Dietrich is a serious, conscientious, scrupulous character. And what care he takes of his troops! He's a phenomenon in the class of people like Frundsberg, Ziethen and Seydlitz. He's a Bavarian Wrangel, someone irreplaceable. For the German people Sepp Dietrich is a national institution. For me personally there is the fact that he is one of my oldest companions in the struggle.'

54

In 1956 Dietrich stood trial in Munich charged with the murder of Ernst Röhm, but was acquitted.

If such a guard unit was to have any practical value it had to be militarily trained, and so Himmler was obliged to turn to the Army and police to provide barracks, training facilities and instructors. In view of the Army's anxiety at the attitude of the vast SA (of which the SS still formed a small part) it is surprising that it was prepared to co-operate with the Nazis, but in 1933 the German Army was even more worried about defending Germany's frontiers from foreign encroachment, than the tub-thumping of the SA. In the SA, the Army saw a useful pool of personnel, and it agreed to undertake the military training of selected SA leaders and men, and to make available weapons from the many clandestine dumps in which arms had been concealed from the Allied disarmament commissions.

But the army preferred to deal with the SS, which was smaller and better disciplined. Had the army decided not to pass on its expertise to the SS at this critical time, it is doubtful if the *Waffen-SS* would have ever seen the light of day.

In Hamburg, Dresden, Munich, Ellwangen and Arolsen and other towns *Sonderkommandos* were set up by the SS regional leader. Personnel were volunteers from the *Allgemeine-SS* and other formations of the Nazi Party, while many of the leaders were active or retired officers from the army and police. They injected a military spirit into the *Sonderkommandos* which Himmler found dangerous and tried particularly hard, unsuccessfully, to combat.

The *Stabswache* in Berlin was in the strange position of carrying out the official function of guarding the Head of State, while remaining a party organization. It was to overcome this constitutional anomaly and to invest the *Stabswache* with executive powers that the unit was moved to the police barracks at Berlin Lichterfelde, and placed at the disposition of the Prussian *Land* Police (*Landespolizei*) as the Special Commando Berlin for Special Duties (*Sonderkommando Berlin zur besonderen Verwendung*) in October 1933.

The cost of maintaining this unit would be undertaken by the Ministry of the Interior so to all intents and purposes these SS men became civil servants. In September 1933 at the Reich Party Day Rally in Nuremburg the *Sonderkommando* became the *Adolf Hitler Standarte*, and one month later on 9 November its men swore a personal oath of Allegiance to Adolf Hitler.

At the beginning of 1934 the Political Readiness Squads were still desperately short of weapons and uniforms, while motor transport was virtually non-existent. They were considered to be fit only for riot control and the liquidation of political opponents. In June 1934 that is exactly what they were called upon to do.

At the beginning of June 1934 Himmler began to act against the SA, but it was not until the third week of June that SS units all over Germany were placed on an alert and all leave was cancelled. On 30 June 'Sepp' Dietrich and part of Adolf Hitler's personal regiment, now called the *Leibstandarte* (Bodyguard Regiment) *Adolf Hitler*, moved to Munich which was expected to be the centre of SA resistance. Other detachments of the *Leibstandarte* were sent to guard the offices of the Gestapo and SD, and other SS installations and important government and party buildings against an SA attack.

Throughout Germany Gestapo and SD officers were ordered to arrest all those whose names appeared on specially prepared lists, and soon SS execution squads in Berlin and Munich were loading their guns. In Berlin-Lichterfelde *Leibstandarte* firing squads were busy for several days as they despatched over 150 victims including the leader of the Berlin SA, Karl Ernst. In the Stadelheim Prison in Munich the Chief of Staff of the SA, Ernst Röhm, was shot dead by Theodor Eicke and his adjutant Michael Lippert.

By the 20 July things had returned to normal in Berlin-Lichterfelde, but the sanguinary events which had taken place there were remembered by Heinrich Himmler at a speech he gave in Posen in 1943:

'On 30 June 1934 we did not hesitate to do the duty we had

been ordered to do and stand lapsed comrades up against the wall and shoot them. We have never talked about it amongst ourselves – it appalled everyone – and yet we all knew that if it became necessary, and similar orders were given, it would be done again.'

All the warring factions seemed pleased with the outcome of the purge of the SA. Hitler had rid himself of an embarrassment, the SS had achieved independence and the Army was rid of a dangerous rival without having had to dirty its hands. So pleased was the Army that on 5 July 1934 the Minister of Defence offered the SS enough weapons to equip a complete division. Little did the Army realize that in the very moment in which it was rid of the SA, a far more dangerous rival in the shape of the SS had emerged.

On 24 September 1934 the chiefs of the Armed Forces were advised that Hitler, after detailed discussions with the *Reichsführer-SS* had agreed to the formation of the SS Special Disposal Troops (*SS-Verfügungstruppe* or SS-VT). The document reminded them that 'the SS is a political organization of the NSDAP, and has neither the weapons, military organization nor training to carry out its political tasks. The SS is unarmed and organized from a political point of view. In order to be able to carry out the special internal tasks allotted to it by the Führer the following changes are to take place.

'The SS is to form a regular armed Special Disposal Troop of three infantry regiments (organized and equipped like those of the Army) and a signals battalion. The formation of further units so that the SS-VT can be deployed as a division will be done with the approval of the Reich Defence Minister.

'The SS-VT is subordinate to the *Reichsführer-SS* but in wartime it will be placed under Army command. In peacetime there is no organizational link between the SS-VT and the German Army.

'The SS-VT will be formed from volunteers who sign on for four years, and up to 25,000 men will no longer be liable for military service since time served in the SS-VT counts as military service for conscription purposes. Pay and conditions are to be those of the Army, but costs will be borne by the Reich Ministry of the Interior.

'Officers, who may sign on for longer than four years, will be trained in one of the three new SS officers' academies.'

Although the Army had been content to allow the SS a few lightly armed squads, an SS infantry division was quite another matter. Such a formation not only impinged on the Army's privileged position as 'sole weapon bearers of the Nation', but it also struck at the very roots of the Army's existence, and henceforth the Army grew increasingly suspicious of what it called the 'asphalt soldiers'. This name had come about because of the black uniforms, and the very frequent appearance of SS troops at ceremonial occasions.

By the time the Political Readiness Squads had been removed from the control of the SS Regional Leaders, and brought together as the *SS-Verfügungstruppe*, with its own inspectorate in October 1936, the armed SS had split. The SS-VT was formed from the *Leibstandarte Adolf Hitler* and the various *Politische Bereitschaften*, but one of them – *SS-Sonderkommando 3* – became a guard unit for the concentration camp at Weimar-Buchenwald, and so became a part of Theodor Eicke's SS Deaths Head units (*SS-Totenkopfverbände*).

Eicke was continuously drumming into his men that they formed a distinct branch of the SS with their own organization, tasks and *esprit*, but the small guard detachments were growing in quality and quantity and becoming increasingly militarized, so that when war came in 1939 the *SS-Totenkopfverbände* were able to take their place alongside the Army, and in due course became one of the best divisions of the *Waffen-SS*, whose personnel won more Knights Crosses (equivalent to the British Victoria Cross) than any other *Waffen-SS* division. The personnel for the original *Sonderkommandos* were specially selected volunteers from the *Allgemeine-SS* and other party formations, although party membership was never obligatory. Men had to be Aryans of good character (no police record) and have a minimum height of 1.72 metres. Young men came forward to join for different reasons. Some were looking for nothing more than a regular job at a time when the country was far from complete recovery from the aftermath of the economic collapse, while others joined like Wolff Sendele because:

'In those days there was no Waffen-SS yet, it was the *Politische Bereitschaft Württemberg* as the unit was called, and since we were all volunteers, I'd hoped that we would be able to achieve what we had envisaged – what we wanted to be – a fighting force which would be able to get to grips with things, that it would become a disciplined, organized force, which is what we had envisaged before 1933.'

There was no shortage of volunteers, as young boys – mostly from rural areas – longed to put on the smart black uniform and join an elite unit. Himmler remembered that 'in those days we assembled the most magnificent Aryan manhood in the *SS-Verfügungstruppe*. We even turned down a man if he had one tooth filled.'

While the rank and file presented no problems to Himmler, he was obliged to accept into the SS a number of experienced Army and police officers and non-commissioned officers as instructors and unit commanders, who, if not openly anti-Nazi, were disinterested in the political role of the SS in the Nazi state. It was they who injected into the SS-VT a strong military spirit, which Himmler found so dangerous, and which he tried unsuccessfully to combat.

The man chosen by Himmler to organize and train the SS-VT was the fifty-six-year-old former Reichswehr Major-General Paul Hausser. Hausser's first task was to set up two academies in which the future officer corps of the SS-VT could be trained along tried and tested Reichswehr lines but with strong SS racial, physical and political overtones. The resulting establishments have been described as a cross between the Spartan Hoplites and the Guards' Depot at Caterham.

Having formed the first SS officers' academy in Brunswick,

59

Hausser moved to Berlin in the latter part of 1934 to set up the SS-VT inspectorate, and on 1 October 1936 he was appointed inspector. Although Hausser typified the traditional Prussian Junker officer he was sufficiently imaginative to see that in the SS-VT he had the opportunity to create a new type of armed force grounded on well-tried Reichswehr principles, but incorporating many new ideas.

Over and above the strict SS selection procedures insisted upon by Himmler's race office, Hausser chose his future officers on the basis of character and ability, rather than on class, background or educational qualification. As many as 40 per cent of the pre-war SS-trained officers had only elementary school education.

Whereas the revolutionary thinkers of the German Army were experimenting with highly mobile armoured formations, the SS concentrated on the physical quality of its personnel. One of the SS-VT's commanders was Felix Steiner who had served in the trenches in World War I, and remembered the small assault troops which had carried out lightning raids on the enemy trenches and often scored spectacular successes with comparatively few casualties, and he and some of the other SS-VT commanders looked upon the SS-VT as an experimental force in which new tactics, equipment and weapons could be developed. Richard Schulze-Kossens remembers that the SS-VT was made up of 'Volunteers who had been specially selected for their height and athletic prowess. It was a selected troop of fine men who underwent a particularly hard and thorough training. So obviously one could get them to do things in their training that one couldn't do with ordinary soldiers. We felt ourselves to be a sort of experimental troop. For example we were the first soldiers ever to wear camouflage jackets – and the Army laughed at us. They said, "you're running around like tree frogs; real soldiers wear field-grey".'

The blind fervour of a growing generation of Hitler Youths together with the reforming zeal of ex-officer heretics like Felix Steiner combined with a certain dynamism and the traditional arrogance of an imperial guard, to produce a sense of mission and superiority which was the hallmark of the pre-war armed SS.

On 17 August 1938 the *SS-Verfügungstruppe* having played a minor role in the annexation of Austria, after which a fourth regiment was formed from Austrians for both the SS-VT and SS-TV, was placed under the command of the Army High Command.

The final peacetime order-of-battle of the SS-VT was as follows:

UNIT	GARRISON
Headquarters Staff	Berlin
Motorized Regiment *Leibstandarte SS Adolf Hitler*	
Regiment *Deutschland*	Munich
Regiment *Germania*	Hamburg
Regiment *Der Führer*	Vienna, Graz and Klagenfurt
Regimental Staff 'N' commanding two motorcycle battalions	Nuremberg
Motorized Engineer Battalion	Dresden
Motorized Signal Battalion	Berlin
Medical Battalion	Berlin

Personnel strength in August 1938 was 28,460 all ranks. In May 1939 SS regiment *Deutschland* commanded by *SS-Standartenführer* (colonel) Felix Steiner arranged an exercise at the Münsterlager manœuvre area. Richard Schulze-Kossens: 'Let me give you an example of why we considered ourselves to be elite soldiers. In 1939 we carried out a regimental exercise with live ammunition in the presence of Adolf Hitler, four generals and the Minister of War. This meant that the whole regiment was under fire from artillery, infantry, marksmen, sub-machine guns, hand grenades and flame-throwers. That had never been done in the German Army before, and you can only do that sort of thing with volunteers who have been particularly well trained.'

SS and Police 1933–1945

In its final form the Greater German Reich
will encompass within its frontiers groups of
people who at the outset are not necessarily well
disposed to the State. It is therefore necessary
to maintain a militarised State Police force
capable of representing and implementing the
internal authority of the Reich.

ADOLF HITLER

In the chapter dealing with the Gestapo and SD it has been described how the SS leadership took over one by one the political departments of the *Land* police forces, and finally the Prussian Gestapo. The SS then began the process of removing the *Land* police forces from federal control and placing them at the disposal of the Nazi State, not as an organisation for the passive protection of the constitution, but as an offensive instrument for the destruction of all political and social opposition to the Nazi regime. The first step in the *Reichification* of the police was the 30 January 1934 'Law for the Reconstruction of the Reich' which unified the police under the authority of the Prussian Ministry of the Interior, which in November 1934 became the Reich Ministry of the Interior. In June 1936 Himmler became *Reichsführer-SS* and Chief of the German Police in the Reich Ministry of the Interior, but he did not become Minister of the Interior himself until late in the war. Anyway he could now set about creating a Reich police force which would be totally integrated with the SS in what he referred to as the State Protection Corps. This integration took place on both administrative and personnel levels.

At the top Himmler severed, one by one, all constitutional

links between the police and the national, as opposed to political, government. Despite Minister of the Interior Frick's frequent complaints to Hitler about the independence of his subordinate Himmler, he was told by Hitler to give the *Reichsführer-SS* as free a hand as possible because, according to Hitler, 'the police was in good shape under Himmler's command'.

Himmler set in motion four fundamental changes within the German police. The separate *Land* police forces became a Reich police force with unified command structure, organization and uniforms. This national police force was removed from governmental (i.e. constitutional) control. It was then divided into a uniformed branch (*Ordnungspolizei*) and plain clothes branch (*Sicherheitspolizei*) into which was incorporated the criminal police, and finally this new police force was to be fully incorporated into the SS.

In pre-war Germany Himmler had to contend with a veritable jungle of conflicting power bases which made his task of setting up the ultimate Police State almost impossible. Even the Führer, while appreciating Himmler's loyalty and organizational talents, was careful not to allow him to become *too* powerful. The Nazi Party leadership jealously guarded its powers against encroachments by the SS. And finally there were the federal governments which clung to the last vestiges of their rapidly evaporating authority. Himmler had no choice but to accept this situation in the old Reich, but he was careful to create the framework for absolute SS power in the newly acquired territories. In November 1937 he ordered that in the event of mobilization, the post of Senior SS and Police Commander (*Höhere-SS und Polizeiführer* – HSSPF) would be created. The HSSPF was to be Himmler's representative in the field of political administration in the occupied territories, and was to co-ordinate the deployment of the SS, police, security police and SD in the carrying out of the special duties allotted to him by Himmler.

In the occupied territories under Military Government the HSSPF was subordinated to the Army in all questions relating to movement, supplies and accommodation, and the Army was to be kept advised of all security actions, and could order them to be halted if they interfered with military operations. However, SS and police personnel were subject to SS and police law.

In the occupied territories the HSSPF held considerable power, and in Poland even took a hand in drafting executive police laws. They not only handled all security matters appertaining to the SS and police, but had on their staffs SS officials responsible for racial affairs, resettlement, emigration, migration and Germanization. They thus became completely involved in the administration and supervision of the killing operations undertaken by the SS and police, particularly in Poland.

By January 1944 there were nineteen HSSPFs in the Reich (including one for the Government General in Poland), and fourteen Senior and two Supreme (*Höchste-SS und Polizeiführer*) SS and Police Commanders in the occupied territories.

On the personnel level the incorporation of the German Police into the SS Order with its strict racial and physical standards presented both the SS and police leadership with a number of problems which were never completely resolved. The police had been in the forefront of the Weimar Republic's struggle against radical political parties which, of course, had included the National Socialists. Although as former soldiers many policemen tended to favour the Nazis, there was little love lost between them and the police.

While purging the police of all its unreliable elements, the SS seduced the rest with the promise of enhanced prestige, increased funds, smart new uniforms and unlimited police powers. At the 1937 Nuremberg Rally Hitler addressed the first police contingent to take part in a Nazi Party congress as follows: 'The German police will be brought into increasingly active association with the movement which not only represents present day Germany, but its image and its leader.' But the police was careful to retain intact its excellent *ésprit* and traditions, and in fact conceded far less to the SS than the SS conceded to it.

German policemen who came up to SS recruiting standards were allowed, and in some cases pressurized, to become members of the *Allgemeine-SS* with the same rank as they held in the police. But Himmler also reserved for himself the right to widen the circle of policemen who might be accepted into the SS. Once accepted, policemen serving in the plain clothes branches of the police were to wear SS uniform, when a uniform was required, while policemen in the uniformed branch (*Ordnungspolizei*) were to wear the SS runes (the emblem of the SS) on the left side of the police tunic.

Before World War I most German policemen were former soldiers who had completed their term of service and wanted employment in the civil service. This trend not only continued during the Weimar Republic but was expanded as a result of the Versailles Treaty which restricted the size of the German Army to 100,000 men. Those soldiers for whom there was no place in the Army were transferred to the police which was increasing its military capacity because of the unsettled political situation in Germany at that time.

The Army approved of this militarization of the police because it relieved the Army of the necessity of having to put down civil disorders, and at the same time created a pool of trained personnel which would be available to the Army when the time came for unrestricted expansion. From 1933 there was an intensification of military training in the police units, so that when in 1935 conscription was re-introduced the police was able to transfer to the German Army over sixty thousand fully trained men, many of whom were of non-commissioned officer and officer calibre.

Thereafter, and bearing in mind the existence of the armed SS, the *Ordnungspolizei* maintained only a few armed units which were organized in groups (*Gruppen*) and battalions (*Abteilungen*) which were motorized and armed mostly with obsolete light infantry weapons. Police units participated in the annexation of Austria and in the occupation of Czecho-slovakia, but the *Ordnungspolizei* headquarters had not en-visaged that the police would be called upon to form battle-worthy units for regular deployment in the front line or against large bands of partisans in the rear areas. At the beginning of the war the *Ordnungspolizei* had 121,000 men available for policing duties and for special tasks in the war zone. The call-up of reservists – most of whom were either too old or too young for military service – raised police strength to 224,500 men, 1,376 officers and 57,800 men who were organized in one hundred and one police battalions. A further 475 officers and 15,328 men went to form the SS-Police division.

Soon after the beginning of World War II German police units were thrown into action at Kutno near Lodz, where a particularly serious situation had developed as a result of a Polish counter-attack, but in the main their efforts were directed at restoring law and order as soon as the tide of war had passed. German policemen rounded up and disarmed stragglers, took over police stations and prisons, collected and guarded abandoned military equipment and provided sentries for important buildings, works and factories.

In the occupied territories the police units constituted the main armed force at the disposal of the HSSPF and were employed by him for many and varied tasks. The most serious threat developing in the occupied territories, particularly those in eastern and South-eastern Europe, was the increase in armed attacks against German military personnel. As the scale of partisan activity increased so did the degree of sav-agery of German reprisals. Police units took a leading part in sweeps and searches in partisan-infested areas and any farm-ers or villagers suspected of helping the partisans were either shot on the spot or taken as hostages and their homes burnt to the ground. It was inevitable that during these 'cleansing operations' the police came across various categories of 'un-desirables' such as Jews, gypsies and the occasional Com-munist official. Police units also provided the firing squads for the execution of hostages and those sentenced to death by special courts.

Typical of the telex messages which poured into Himmler's headquarters is the following from HSSPF of Southern Russia SS General Hanz Prützmann dated 21 August 1941: 'Police Regiment South led an "action" in the forested area of Dilka and Domanka during which Police Battalion 45 shot five prisoners, three of whom were poachers, nineteen partisans and sixty-six Jews, and at Sudilkov a further four hundred and seventy-one Jews.'

Rather than conceal their murderous activities police commanders fell over themselves in the race to run up the highest score, and they were not loath to exaggerate the number of their victims if they thought Himmler might be impressed by their zeal.

It must be remembered that these terrible crimes were not committed by Nazi fanatics from the pre-war SS, but by ordinary, often elderly German policemen who had been brought up in an authoritarian society and had succumbed to that particularly German weakness of carrying out, without question, any order given to them by a superior. This does not mean that many Policemen were not disgusted by what they had to do, but only very few had the courage to refuse. The Federal German Senior Chief State Prosecutor Alfred Spiess, who has made a detailed study of SS and police crimes in Poland, remembers a case which was reported in the Treblinka trial.

'One morning an SS and police unit which included reservists got the order to shoot women and children in a neighbouring village. In this unit was a clerk from Frankfurt who had been called up as a police reservist. When he heard this order he took one step forward and said "I'm not putting my hand to this – it is a crime, and I'm not going to do it." He was bawled out and sent away, but nothing happened to him. He wasn't brought before an SS and police court and was left unharmed. Since we had come across other similar cases we discussed this question with former SS judges at the

Treblinka trial. Why were these people not brought before an SS and police court? The explanation was very simple. If these people had been brought before an SS and police court, it would have to establish which order had been disobeyed. What sort of order was it? In one case it would have been an order for the mass-murder of Jews, and in another the shooting of women and children. But these were both criminal orders, and according to the Military Penal Code, paragraph 47, clause 3, which was still valid in those days, a soldier was not obliged to carry out a criminal order. You see, that meant that this Military Penal Code was also applicable to the SS and police, and so when a man is brought before a court, the court has to ascertain if the order was criminal and who gave the order. One would have found the chain of command ending up with Hitler himself – and that was simply out of the question, wasn't it?'

Heinrich Himmler 1900–1945

It is the curse of the great to have to walk
over corpses

H.HIMMLER

In his introduction to my *Pictorial History of the SS*, Professor Hugh Trevor Roper described the SS as 'the engine of terror without which Nazism would not have been itself and Hitler might never have solidified his power'. The SS was no doubt a powerful driving force which crashed Germany through the barrier of rationalism and civilized restraint. The man who stoked the boilers of that engine was Heinrich Himmler and the fuel, of his own concoction, was a mixture of fervently held national aspirations supercharged with racism and coated with a veneer of perverted militarism.

What sort of man was Heinrich Himmler? When Karl Wolff first met him in 1931, he found him 'a great disappointment; his whole bearing was rather sly and unmilitary'. The Englishman Stephen Roberts described Himmler as 'a man of exquisite courtesy and still interested in the simple things of life. He has none of the pose of those Nazis who act as demigods ... No man looks less like his job than this police dictator of Germany.' Major-General Walther Dornberger, who was in charge of Germany's rocket development which was taken over by the SS in 1944, thought Himmler looked like 'an intelligent elementary school-teacher, certainly not a man of violence'.

But Himmler was also a pedantic, romantically eccentric,

petty bourgeois, who, according to another contemporary observer 'made himself sinister by his capacity to concentrate upon trivia, his pettifogging conscientiousness and his inhuman methodology; he had the touch of a robot'. Himmler was also motivated by a slavish devotion to his Führer which was certainly obsessive, but although Hitler respected the abilities of his *Treue Heinrich* he never warmed to him and Himmler never became a member of Hitler's intimate inner circle. In fact Himmler was a very ordinary offspring of a typical middle-class Bavarian Catholic family. His father had been tutor to Prince Heinrich of Bavaria, and young Heinrich was named after his auspicious godfather. His mother was the daughter of a Savoyard greengrocer. Like most young Germans of his class and background, Himmler's first ambition was to become a soldier, but that was frustrated by the ending of the war. He had always shown an interest in plants and herbs and so he enrolled at the Technical High School of Munich University where he read for an agricultural diploma. Freed from family restraints Himmler entered the student life of the Bavarian capital with vigour and soon acquired a reputation for being friendly, helpful, studious and a bit of a bore. He joined the student association Apollo, so that he could receive the coveted duelling scars, but found the excessive beer-drinking played havoc with his delicate constitution.

After qualifying in August 1922 Himmler started work in an agricultural chemical works, but he still had not given up the idea of becoming a soldier, and so he joined the *Kriegsflagge*, a nationalist para-military organization, commanded by the retired Captain Ernst Röhm. The lure of a soldier's life proved too much for Himmler, holding down a boring job in Schleissheim, and he returned to Munich in time to play a minor role in the Hitler putsch in November 1923. The putsch was a failure, Hitler was thrown into prison and the Nazi Party banned. Himmler with two failed careers behind him yearned to belong to something or someone, but to what and to whom he did not know.

Despite the failure of the Munich putsch, Himmler decided to stay in politics and became a propagandist for the National Socialist Freedom Movement – one of the two warring factions – formed from the remnants of the Nazi Party in lower Bavaria. During the run-up to the 1924 elections for the *Reichstag* Himmler began to identify himself with the atmosphere of resentment and prevalent anti-Semitism and anti-freemasonry of the German nationalist movements. Himmler's demagogy so appealed to the Catholic peasantry that his party won two million votes and thirty-two seats in the *Reichstag*. In December 1924 Hitler was released from prison and within a couple of months had united the various Bavarian *Völkisch** and National Socialist parties in the NSDAP.

The philosophy which Himmler was in the process of formulating sprang from his interest in ancient German history, which he had inherited from his schoolmaster father, coupled with a fashionable dislike of industrialization and urbanization. These beliefs were also held by the *Völkisch* movement and the *Artamanen* who were nationalistic idealists obsessed with the romantic idea of the simple healthy existence of the settler and his struggle against the ancient Slav enemy. Himmler became an *Artaman* and soon became one of its leaders in Bavaria. Another *Artaman* in Brandenburg was the future commandant of Auschwitz, Rudolf Höss.

In his memoirs Höss describes the *Artamanen* as a 'community of young people of both sexes, who had the interests of their country at heart. They came from the youth movements of all the nationalist-inclined and were people who all, at one time or another, had wanted to escape from the unhealthy, dissolute and superficial life of the towns and especially large cities, and to discover for themselves a healthy, tough but natural way of life on the land. They did not drink or smoke, and forswore everything that did not contribute to the healthy development of their minds and bodies. They wanted,

*See footnote p. 28.

furthermore, to return to the soil from which their forefathers had sprung, and to settle on the land which had given birth to the nation.'

Contained within these innocent-sounding aims were the germs of the destructive ideals which the SS put into action fifteen years later. To the SS the unhealthy, debilitating and superficial quality of town life was due to the 'cosmopolitan' influence of Jewry and international freemasonry, while the soil of their forefathers, to which they longed to return, was now inhabited by Slavs.

At the beginning of his political career Himmler spent all his time rushing around Bavaria on a motorcycle addressing meetings and building up the Nazi Party. His hard work and organizing ability did not go unrewarded and in 1925 he rose from deputy *Gauleiter* for Upper Bavaria/Swabia to deputy Chief of Reich Propaganda and then deputy Reich Leader of the SS. These grand titles seem to have gone to young Himmler's head and in party headquarters he soon earned himself a reputation for taking himself rather too seriously. Behind his back the toughs in Hitler's *chauffeureska* made fun of the pallid, clerk-like young man whom they called 'pince-nez Heini' and 'poor fish'.

In July 1928 Himmler married and the couple purchased a smallholding at Waldtrudering near Munich, where they planned to make a living breeding chickens. But Himmler was so involved in party work that he spent little time at home, and this together with financial problems soon put a severe strain on the marriage.

On 6 January 1929 Himmler became Reich Leader of the whole SS, which at that time had just two hundred and eighty members. Undeterred by the scorn of his comrades, Himmler immediately set to work to increase both the strength and influence of the SS and in April submitted the first draft of what was eventually to become the Order of the SS. Himmler saw the SS as an elite founded on the principles of strict selection on the basis of race and appearance rather than on intellectual excellence. As early as 1929 Himmler considered weeding out the existing SS and ridding it of all impurities, 'like a gardener weeding a flower bed', but he realized that it was not the time to implement such drastic action. Instead he increased the strength of the SS from one thousand in December 1929 to fifty thousand in March 1933 when Hitler came to power. Although he still insisted on strict enrolment procedures for new members, only those who could prove Aryan ancestry back to 1800 (officers 1750) were accorded the ultimate privilege which Himmler could bestow on his SS men – the right to sire the future generations of pure SS men.

Having laid down the rules for acceptance into the SS, Himmler now turned his attention to the women his SS men were marrying, and he found them far from suitable. In December 1931 he introduced the SS Marriage Order which every SS man had to swear to uphold. The SS man and his fiancée had to fill in an SS Race Office form and supply the required proof of Aryan ancestry and photographs of his bride and himself in bathing costume. They were carefully scrutinized for traces of racial impurity. Once accepted and married the bride entered her name in the SS Clan Book (*SS-Sippenbuch*) and was permitted – or rather encouraged – to have children. The strict scrutiny of marriage applications brought to Himmler's attention many cases of SS men – even one of the first like Emil Maurice – who had Jewish ancestry and in the years 1934–36, fifty thousand men were released from the SS because they did not conform to Himmler's ideal. This Marriage Order was one of the most unpopular and flaunted of all SS regulations, and many SS men left the SS rather than submit to interference in what they considered to be one of the most fundamental personal rights left to man – the right to marry whomever they wished.

Himmler had been brought up in the Catholic faith but when he went up to Munich University he became increasingly detached from the Church, and then decidedly anti-Christian. As he evolved his fantastic concept of the SS as a sort of ancient Teutonic Order, he deliberately put pressure on SS men to leave the Church and become 'believers in

God'. But despite his attempts to create a distinctive SS ideology, he failed to capture the imagination of the average SS man with his hollow hotch-potch of neo-Paganism and cult of ancestor worship, so that only one in three SS men renounced their Christian faith. Only in the armed SS and SS Death's Head units did 'believers in God' become a slight majority. In the SS calendar the Christian festivals and ceremonies were replaced by neo-Pagan feasts and rituals in celebration of the changing of the seasons. The main festivals were the summer and winter solstices, when the sun reaches its maximum distance from the equator. Then there were the harvest festival and festival of death which was held in November. Himmler even tried to replace the traditional Christmas festivities, but SS families still continued to celebrate it in the traditional way.

The SS tended to accept Himmler's *Ersatzreligion* more readily in summer than in winter, and Karl Wolff tells an amusing story of the celebration of a winter solstice. 'Himmler dragged us up the Brocken [the highest peak in the Harz mountains celebrated in many ancient German legends] in a sledge. It was so cold that both horses – and they were heavy drays – developed a kidney colic and just stopped and stood there unable to go on; it was a dreadful affair. At the top of the mountain there was a huge bonfire and after it had been lit Himmler gave a speech on the theme of the family as the oven of the people. But there was such a wind up there that we were all half frozen and longed for him to hurry up and get it over with, so we could get to a pub, defrost and warm ourselves up a bit. That certainly wasn't a very good advertisement for a new religion, was it?'

Christmas was to be celebrated on 21 December and marriages no longer took place in church, but in an SS building in winter or under a lime tree in summer. Flowers were replaced by decorations incorporating the life runes, sunflowers and fir twigs. An eternal flame burned in an urn in front of which the couple exchanged rings and received the official SS gift of bread and salt which was arranged on a wooden platter on which was carved 'be worthy of the bread of your own soil then your kin will live for ever'. As in other religions bread and salt were regarded as symbols of the earth's fruitfulness and purity. The legal requirement of signing the register was supplemented by the SS ceremony of signing the SS Clan Book by the bride.

At the name-giving ceremony (christening) the child was wrapped in a shawl of undyed wool embroidered with oak leaves, runcs and swastikas. Both parents placed their hands on the child's head and pronounced fashionable Germanic names. Himmler's personal gift to the first child was a blue shawl and silver beaker and spoon. For every fourth child the parents received a silver candlestick engraved with the legend 'you are just a link in the clan's endless chain'.

The SS couple were expected to produce at least four children, but in fact SS birthrate remained average for the country as a whole. In an attempt to encourage SS families to have more children and to improve the standard of lying-in care, the SS established Well of Life (*Lebensborn*) homes. These were financed by contributions from SS leaders and they were available to both married and unmarried mothers. Despite salacious rumours about them being SS stud farms, only a small percentage of children born in peacetime were illegitimate.

As a young man Himmler had been fascinated with plants and herbs, and after the premature end of his military career, he decided to become a farmer. Thereafter, in his writings and speeches, he always claimed to be a farmer by birth, blood and inclination and although this was not actually true, the SS seemed to have made its greatest impact in the rural areas, and as the sons of farmers flocked to join the SS, it became – particularly in its armed units – an organization of farmers and artisans.

Karl Wolff considers that 'Himmler was obsessed by breeding. He wanted to increase the egg-laying of his hens, to improve animals in general and produce higher-yielding corn, and all sorts of things; he was really a breeding expert.'

The SS became for Himmler the vehicle whereby he could put into practise his obsession, not only with breeding, but also with agriculture. Having become a member of the *Artamanen* Himmler was befriended by an Argentine German called Walther Darré who had been educated in England and served as an official in the Prussian Ministry of Agriculture. Darré was equally obsessed by the *Völkisch* concepts of 'blood and soil' and had authored a number of books on the theme of 'Peasantry as the Prime Source of the Nordic Race' and 'The Breeding Objective of the German Nation'. He acted as a chrysalis to Himmler's equally daft but even vaguer concepts. Darré became agricultural adviser in Himmler's headquarters, where in January 1932 Himmler set up an SS Race Office (later Race and Resettlement Office or *Rasse und Siedlungshauptamt* – RuSHA). The main tasks of this office before the war were the guarding of the ideological and racial purity of all SS members, the racial processing of all applications for SS memberships, and the vetting of SS fiancées. In an attempt to reverse the general trend away from the rural areas Darré's office encouraged SS men to remain on the land, and give assistance to SS men who wanted to settle on the land. To promote racial awareness and to deal with all technical matters relating to agriculture, SS men were appointed as agricultural specialists in SS units in rural areas.

In 1936 Himmler was asked to provide an SS leader to organize an office in the Foreign Ministry to deal with matters relating to ethnic Germans or *Volksdeutsche* living mainly in eastern Europe. The appointment of *SS-Obergruppenführer* (General) Werner Lorenz provided Himmler with a useful *entrée* into the tempting field of foreign relations. From then on the SS became increasingly involved in organizing the German minorities in eastern and south-eastern Europe and fermenting tensions between them and the indigenous populations amongst whom they lived. In the Sudetenland, Poland, Romania and Slovakia the SS was for ever treading on the heels of the Foreign Ministry and the German military intelligence service or *Abwehr*. In 1939 the SS succeeded in provoking the Czechs and Poles into carrying out brutal reprisals against the German minorities and these, together with the mock attack by SS men dressed in Polish uniforms on a German radio station at Gleiwitz, were used as justification for the invasion of Poland on 1 September 1939.

As soon as Poland had been overrun and the first wave of SS terror had abated, Himmler the mass murderer became Himmler the 'nurseryman of the Germanic ideal'. As Reich Commissar for the Strengthening of Germandom he began to organize the repatriation of 120,000 Germans living in the Baltic countries, 136,000 in Soviet-occupied Poland and another 200,000 or more from Romania, Yugoslavia and Slovakia to the Polish territory newly incorporated in the Reich and ruthlessly cleared of its Polish inhabitants. During the bitter winter of 1939–40 130,000 *Volksdeutsche* from Galicia and Volhynia set out on what the Nazi propaganda machine called the final trek. Even as the Germans were suffering their catastrophic defeat at Stalingrad even more ethnic Germans, deep in the Russian hinterland, were being uprooted by the SS and sent westwards for resettlement, a process completed after the war by the Soviet government.

In practical terms the *Volksdeutsche* were needed by Germany to make good a grave shortage of workers in industry, especially after the beginning of the war and mobilization of the German people. But to Himmler it was the beginning of his most grandiose and bizarre project – the remodelling of the whole of eastern Europe. In May 1940 Himmler had submitted to Hitler a top secret 'eyes only' memorandum entitled 'Some thoughts on the treatment of foreign populations in the East'. In Nazi terminology the East meant primarily Poland and the Soviet Union. Himmler's idea was to break up the traditional, national, social, political and cultural infrastructure and extract from it all valuable racial elements which could gradually be Germanized. The rest were to be left with no rights, no education and no opportunities – to wither away as Nazi helots. SS commissions toured Poland investigating not only those of German origin, but also Poles.

The most tragic aspect of this programme was the kidnapping of blond and blue-eyed Polish children who were sent to *Lebensborn* homes for adoption by SS families without children.

In the vastness of the East, Himmler dreamed of creating a Germanic wonderland. It was to be divided into marks, settled by Europeans of Germanic stock, governed by SS-appointed headmen, and protected from the Asiatic hordes by a line of twenty-six strongpoints manned by SS peasant warriors. To commemorate the great sacrifice made by those Germans who died in the biological struggle against the Slavs and to instil in these warrior settlers a fighting spirit which would ensure the indestructibility of their way of life, vast castles of the dead (*Tötenburgen*) would be erected on the sites of the bloodiest land battles.

Despite the appearance of monolithic and unlimited power projected by the SS, Himmler continuously found other party and government agencies cutting across his tracks in the occupied eastern territories. Initially Poland had been under military government, and the generals had tried to limit the worst excesses of the SS. As soon as civil government was introduced in October 1939, Himmler had to contend with old party foes like Dr Hans Frank who had been appointed governor of the Government General, and the East Prussian *Gauleiter* Erich Koch, both of whom were equally anxious to carve out their own empires in the East, independently of the SS.

As certain victory turned to probable defeat Himmler had to close the files on some of his more fantastic schemes and concentrate his energies and organizational talent on winning the war. The Waffen-SS was continuously growing in size and proficiency, and was seen by friends and enemies to be growing to maturity on the eastern front. Inevitably this new military elite grew further and further apart from its spiritual base and its political leader. Himmler was for ever admonishing his Waffen-SS generals, who were a pretty independent lot, for using Army rank titles in preference to their SS ones, saluting in the military as opposed to the Nazi manner, and allowing their men to attend church parades and so on. Felix Steiner, commander of the elite *Wiking* division and one of the Waffen-SS's most brilliant generals dismissed Himmler as a 'sleazy romantic' and carried on as before. Richard Schulze-Kossens remembers that 'Himmler didn't enjoy visiting his troops and used to say to them "you think you're superior and feel more attached to the Army, but don't forget that the Waffen-SS has its roots in the Allgemeine-SS".'

On 25 August 1943 Himmler became Minister of the Interior and could now divest his organization of the last slender threads of restraint imposed upon him by the professional civil servants, but it was really too late because Himmler himself was beginning to have doubts. He still displayed the same fanatical zeal in the service of his *Führer* but in great secrecy two of his most trusted subordinates, Walter Schellenberg, head of the SD, and Karl Wolff, chief of his personal staff, were establishing contacts with the British and American governments to find out their attitude towards negotiating an armistice with a Germany without Hitler.

Even in the Waffen-SS there was disillusionment. It was one thing to be the *Führer*'s praetorian guard and quite another to be squandered in hopeless battles against overwhelming odds just to please their megalomaniacal leader. Within the ranks of the Waffen-SS there was a growing realization that the war in the east could only be won with the popular support of the Soviet people. In the Ukraine the German troops had been greeted as liberators, but they had been followed by the fanatical purveyors of the sub-human (*Untermensch*) philosophy who drove the Ukrainians, White Ruthenians and greater Russians into the arms of the partisans.

At the front the Waffen-SS noticed with alarm the increasing heroism and self-sacrifice of the Red Army. The 'Ivans' had better tanks, equally effective but much simpler weapons, and their tactical and strategic skills were improving daily.

'If all this had been achieved by sub-humans what sort of supermen are we?' they began to ask themselves.

On 20 July 1944 there was an attempt to assassinate Hitler and replace the Nazi regime by a government which would then negotiate an honourable surrender with the Allied powers. The SS performance in the critical hours of the Army revolt was abysmal. It had failed in its primary task of protecting the *Führer*, and then it had reacted so slowly that it was left to the propaganda minister, Josef Goebbels, and an Army unit – the Berlin Guards Regiment – to put down the general's revolt. In the West the Waffen-SS was far too involved in a bloody struggle with the Allies in Normandy to play any significant role, although its loyalty to its *Führer* was no longer unquestioned. Over a thousand members of the Paris SD and Gestapo, including their chief Karl Oberg, meekly allowed themselves to be placed under Army arrest, and when released a few hours later held a champagne party for their former captors. When Himmler had recovered from the shock of the attempt itself, evidence soon came to light that implicated members of his very own Gestapo in the plot. The savagery of SS/SD counter-measures which resulted in widespread torture and the deaths of five thousand victims, smacks of a desperate face-saving exercise.

The day after the bomb plot Himmler took over the duties of one of the chief plotters, General Friedrich Fromm, as Chief of the Replacement (*Ersatz*) Army. This was a vital appointment because it controlled virtually the whole German Army, except that part actually engaged at the fronts. It meant that Army personnel, reserve units, training establishments and schools, depots, works, hospitals and prisoner of war camps as well as experimental projects such as the rocket programme, came under SS control. Himmler had now reached the zenith of his power: 'he was lord of the SS – next to the Party the most important organization in the Third Reich; he controlled the police and the Secret Service; he was in charge of the Ministry of the Interior; as the Reich Commissar for the Strengthening of Germandom he was responsible for the regime's racial policy; he supervised relations between the Reich and Nazi movements in the so-called Germanic countries and thirty-eight Waffen-SS divisions owed allegiance to him'.

But rather than remain by his *Führer's* side at these difficult times and protect his vast interests from the jealous machinations of his old party enemies, Himmler allowed himself to be manœuvred into a 'no win' situation. His appointment as Chief of the Replacement Army had re-kindled in him his childhood ambition to become a soldier and despite the advice of his advisers and the horrified dismay of the military High Commander, he accepted command of a German Army Group on the upper Rhine. Under the circumstances he didn't do too badly and so when appointed to command an Army Group on the Vistula, Himmler confidently went to the eastern front to help stem the asiatic hordes 'a situation our ancestors have faced a hundred times in battle against the Avars, Mongols, and in the south-east the Turks and Tartars'. It was hopeless and having committed his best SS units to no avail, he left the mess to the professionals and retired to a sick bed to contemplate the future.

With an almost unbelievable lack of realism Himmler was still convinced that only he – Germany's greatest mass murderer – could negotiate with the Western Allies and bring the war to a swift and advantageous end. As it happened Himmler was in possession of a trump card but he was slow to spot it in his hand and wracked by indecision played it too late. The ultimate fate of the vast concentration camp population – 714,211 in January 1945 – had now become a pawn in a macabre game of poker between negotiators anxious to save as many lives as possible, SS men with their eye on the future who wanted to improve the conditions of the survivors and use them as bargaining counters to extract concessions from the Allies, and the final solution fanatics who were racing against time to murder every Jew they could lay their hands on.

While Himmler was putting on his most civilized face to

impress such distinguished negotiators as Count Folke Bernadotte, his *Wolffchen* (Karl Wolff) was negotiating in secret with the American secret service chief Allen Dulles to arrange the surrender of all Axis forces in Italy. Meanwhile the concentration camps in Silesia and eastern Germany were being evacuated to the west. Diseased, half-starved and emaciated prisoners in filthy striped prison garb or tattered civilian clothes were trudging westwards. Thousands fell by the wayside and were shot as stragglers or left to die, while in packed cattle trucks thousands more were dying of starvation and thirst. Their arrival at camps like Belsen, Buchenwald and Mauthausen led to a complete collapse of the camps routine and organization and to dreadful overcrowding, disease and starvation. The scenes in these camps when liberated by the Allies in April and May 1945 did so much to influence Allied attitudes to Germans in general and the SS in particular after the war was over.

Hitler's unbounded faith in the SS had been badly shaken by the failure of Sepp Dietrich's Sixth Panzer Army's last offensive on Lake Balaton in Hungary in March 1945, and in a fit of spite he ordered his guardsmen to remove their cuffbands (a strip of black cloth on which was embroidered in silver the name of the division) which they so proudly wore on the left sleeve of their uniform tunics. Then in April, while Himmler's secret peace negotiations were in full swing, Hitler retired to his bunker in Berlin where he was to become increasingly isolated from reality. Like his famous predecessor, Fredrick the Great, he waited for the miracle which would save Germany at the eleventh hour. When Felix Steiner's offensive to relieve Berlin was finally aborted it coincided with press reports of the failure of Himmler's secret peace negotiations with the Allies. Hitler was incensed and instead of nominating Himmler as his successor in his political testament, he expelled him from the Nazi Party.

Hitler shot himself in Berlin on 29 April 1945. On 2 May Himmler travelled to northern Germany to join Grand Admiral Dönitz's provisional government at Flensburg. The last thing Dönitz needed was the embarrassing presence of Heinrich Himmler and his formidable entourage. On 3 May Himmler was curtly dismissed but since there was nowhere to go he hung around in an eerie limbo for a fortnight until the Dönitz government was suddenly dissolved by the British.

Rather than presenting himself to the Allies and accepting full responsibility for everything done in his name, he chose to make a futile attempt to escape disguised as a military policeman. On 22 May he was captured by the British and, having identified himself, was searched for poison. When asked to open his mouth he bit on a cyanide capsule and despite the frantic efforts of British intelligence officers and a doctor, Himmler died.

The Waffen-SS 1939–1945

The men of the Waffen-SS were soldiers, like any others!

KONRAD ADENAUER

In the light of Konrad Adenauer's oft-quoted statement and the continuing attempts by Waffen-SS apologists to disassociate the Waffen-SS from the crimes committed by the SS in general, it is necessary to discuss, not so much the military history and organization of the Waffen-SS, but the part it played in Germany's war of conquest and subjugation.

A West German journalist who has made a detailed study of the more recent West German war crimes trials does not believe that 'there was such a thing as a typical SS man. There are indeed well-known cases of Waffen-SS units fighting with chivalry. But because of the training of the SS as a particularly reliable power factor in the Nazi State it produced more criminals than the Army. This was not due to the character of the individual SS man, but rather to the kind of tasks which he was ordered to carry out.'

When the war came in September 1939 there was still no such thing as the Waffen-SS. The armed units of the SS were still divided into the *SS-Verfügungstruppe* and the *SS-Totenkopfverbände* which together comprised a few regiments and guard units with about 28,000 volunteers, but these units did not even constitute one division. By the summer of 1940 these units had become the Waffen-SS with a sixfold increase in manpower. This new 150,000-strong Army was organized in divisions with its own heavy weapons. By the end of the war the Waffen-SS constituted, unofficially, the fourth branch of the *Wehrmacht*** and numbered nearly a million men.

Particularly at the beginning, but also throughout the war, the Waffen-SS was many things to many people. Himmler conceived it as a racially and politically elite military force at the disposal of the *Führer*, but in wartime it had the added advantage of enhancing Himmler's prestige and power within the Nazi hierarchy. Militarily Himmler saw this 'sworn brotherhood of Germanic warriors' as the ideal tool for carving an SS empire out of the vast territory to be seized from the Slavs.

To Hitler the Waffen-SS was to be a new kind of police force uninhibited by the sort of social and constitutional niceties which had affected what he called the 'sock-knitting' police of 1848, or the bureacratized police of 1918. Hitler was loathe to upset the Army by raising up the spectre of a Party Army at such a critical time, and anyway Hitler did not believe the war was going to last for very long. As far as he was concerned the Waffen-SS was to serve at the front for the sole purpose of acquiring sufficient military experience to enable it to represent and implement the authority of the Nazi State both at home and in the newly conquered territories. This new police force or in Nazi jargon State Protection Corps had to prove itself at the front and shed its blood like any Army unit, so that it would then have the moral authority to carry out the special tasks allotted to it. Hitler insisted on quality and not quantity and so for the first two years of the war he restricted the growth of the Waffen-SS to between five and ten per cent of the Army.

The Army looked upon the embryo Waffen-SS with hostility, anxiety and growing envy. The good relations which had prevailed in the mid-1930s between the SS and its Army

* This term is often incorrectly used to mean the German Army when in fact its correct and literal translation is Armed Forces.

instructors had given way to suspicion and mutual antipathy. While acknowledging the excellence of the human material and morale of the SS troops, Army officers saw their increasing military proficiency as a threat.

Of course the young officers of the Waffen-SS were far too involved in their military careers to give much thought to the political implications of their existence. Most Waffen-SS men who served in the pre-war *SS-Verfügungstruppe* remember only the hard physical training, and dismiss the short sessions of political indoctrination as if they were of no consequence. According to Richard Schulze-Kossens 'there was always a gap between Himmler and his soldiers. He wasn't very popular with the men because of his concept of a State Protection Corps, or his ideological ideas about the ancient German tribes and their burial mounds, King Heinrich and all that stuff. We just laughed at it.'

When asked if he, as a member of Adolf Hitler's personal guard regiment, felt any special relationship to Hitler, Hans Wissebach replied 'we didn't consider ourselves to be a guard in the personal sense; you know it was a regiment of over three thousand men. I never shook hands with Hitler. I never had breakfast with him. I only saw him at a distance and that was it. It is true we bore his name [embroidered on the left tunic cuff] and we were of the opinion that we would go into action if ever it became necessary – not for Hitler the man but for Germany. As far as we were concerned, Hitler was the embodiment of the German State in those days.'

Despite the tendency of former Waffen-SS men to dismiss and even ridicule SS ideological training, there is no doubt they fell subconsciously under Hitler's and Himmler's spell. The young men of the pre-war *SS-Verfügungstruppe* had been chosen for their height, Germanic appearance and physical fitness. They were dressed in dramatic black uniforms and continuously appeared in public at ceremonial occasions at which Hitler was often present. These young SS men were idolized by an even younger generation who longed to join the black ranks. The resulting mixture of pride, arrogance

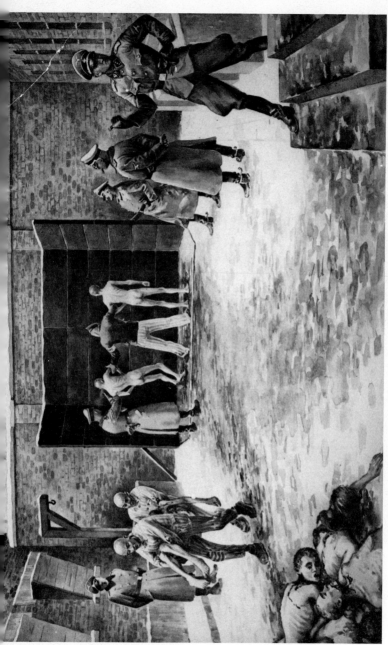

15. An execution outside Block LL in Auschwitz as described in the Thames Television documentary film by former SS guard Kaduk.

16. Göring and his arch-rival Himmler on their way to the Reichstag, September 1932.

17. Execution by police firing squad of Poles rounded up in the 'house cleaning' carried out by the German security forces during the first months of the German occupation.

18. Execution of Soviet citizens accused of being partisans.

19. and 20. Wolf Sendele as an SS man in 1932, and interviewed by Thames Television in Munich in May 1980.

21. SS men baiting Jews in Vienna after the German annexation in March 1938.

22. A young *Waffen-SS* grenadier captured by Canadians during the vicious fighting in Normandy, August 1944. (Keystone)

23. A roll call of inmates from Watenstedt Concentration Camp in Brunswick. These inmates provided slave labour for one of the Hermann Göring Works.

24. A rare photo of four SS guards from Treblinka extermination camp.

25. *SS-Gruppenführer* Philip Bouhler, head of the Führer's personal chancellory and key figure in the Euthanasia Programme.

26. An *Allgemeine-SS* officer and his daughter both conforming exactly to Himmler's Germanic fantasy.

27. SS musicians playing the ancient lurs, 1935.

and devil-may-care cheerfulness* and 'hardness' which characterized the old guard of Waffen-SS men was to prove far stronger than any narrow political fanaticism.

Hardness or *Härte* played a very important part in SS ideology. It equated hardness with manliness as the most important of soldierly qualities. If an SS man was to triumph over his ruthless and sub-human adversaries, he must banish from his mind the old Christian and military concepts of chivalry and compassion which were now equated with weakness. An SS man must be hard not only with himself but with his comrades as well as his enemies. When faced by a situation requiring normal human responses, an SS man might find himself in spiritual conflict with this perverted form of SS militarism, but fearing to appear weak in the eyes of his comrades, he might, against his better judgement, choose the most ruthless solution, because as an SS man that was what was expected of him.

The terrific expansion of the Waffen-SS during the war was realized as a direct result of astute forward planning, which had conceived the pre-war SS-VT and its officers' academies as a nursery for the cultivation of a cadre of well-trained young officers and NCOs. The Army tried to restrict SS recruitment, but the SS's chief recruiter, the Swabian

*'I can assure you that the *Leibstandarte* enjoys an outstanding reputation not only with its superiors but also among its Army comrades. Every division wishes it had the *Leibstandarte* as its neighbour, as much during the attack as in defence. Its inner discipline, its cool dare-devilry, its cheerful enterprise, its unshakeable firmness in a crisis (even when things become difficult or serious), its exemplary toughness, its camaraderie (which deserves special praise) – all these are outstanding and cannot be surpassed. In spite of this the officer corps maintains a pleasant degree of modesty. A genuine elite formation that I am happy and proud to have under my command and, furthermore, one that I sincerely and hopefully wish to retain!'

This is an extract from an unsolicited letter to Himmler from General Eberhard von Mackensen, commander of the Army IIIrd Panzer Corps in praise of the *Leibstandarte*'s conduct during the bitter defensive battles in front of Moscow, in the first winter of the war on the eastern front.

Gottlob Berger, was able to circumvent Army recruitment channels, and with cunning and complete unscrupulousness was able to get all the recruits he needed, although they were not always willing recruits.

Once the war started the Waffen-SS ceased to be a small elite force of hand-picked volunteers, and became – apart from its uniform and the influence of its pre-war personnel – almost indistinguishable from the German Army. Himmler was reluctant to dilute his precious order, but exigencies of war and colossal Waffen-SS losses forced him to accept into the Waffen-SS almost anyone he could get, although he was very adept at finding some ideological formula to justify the intake first of *Volksdeutsche* (ethnic Germans), then volunteers from the so-called 'Germanic' countries, then Moslems from the Balkans, Balts from the Baltic countries of Latvia and Estonia, and finally Slavs and even Tartars.

The outbreak of World War II forced the SS to split once more. The three pillars of Himmler's State Protection Corps before the war were the SS, Police and the Concentration Camps. During the war the *Allgemeine-SS* shrank from its peak strength in 1939 of 250,000 to 40,000 by the end of the war. Most of the pre-war *Allgemeine-SS* men were liable for military service, and while some of them joined the Waffen-SS, by far the largest number served in the armed forces. The German police also had a very important role earmarked for it by Himmler in the occupied territories, but more about that later.

The SS-VT and the SS-TV (Death's Head units) officially became the Waffen-SS in December 1939, although it was not until April 1941 that these earlier names for the armed SS were officially dropped. But here again it was not that simple because what actually happened was that for the first two years of the war there were two Waffen-SS's.

In return for Army cooperation in the building up of the armed SS, Hitler and Himmler had to concede Army operational control of the Waffen-SS in time of war, but they were sufficiently cunning to create the basis for another Waffen-

SS to take the place of the first, so that at no time would the Nazi State be without its own armed protection. This second Waffen-SS was euphemistically called *Polizeiverstärkung* (police reinforcements) and the idea behind it was that on mobilization up to 50,000 SS reservists would be called up to reinforce the existing police which, without the back-up of the *SS-Verfügungstruppe*, would be hard-pressed to put down any serious internal disorders.

The motorized units of the armed SS were distributed amongst German Army formations for the invasion of Poland, and the German Army, still in the process of changing over from horse-power to motor vehicles, was pleased to get the additional motorized units, even if they were from the SS. After observing the SS units in action the Army was not very impressed. SS officers had tried to make up for lack of experience by storming ahead regardless of losses, and any successes had been paid for with a disproportionately high cost in casualties. SS soldiers had also shown a ruthlessness and fanaticism which Army observers found alien to the German military tradition. The SS retorted that the Army out of spitefulness had often given the SS troops impossible tasks and then failed to provide adequate support. The SS was determined that the next time its troops went into action they would form SS divisions with SS artillery and, in the future, SS armour.

The period from September 1939 until May 1940 was a critical one in the development of the Waffen-SS, and it is necessary to understand how it was possible for Himmler to create three SS divisions in less than nine months. It must be remembered that this was done 'under the counter' for while Himmler was trying to expand the Waffen-SS, both Adolf Hitler and the German Army were trying to restrict its growth. Hitler was convinced that the war would not last long, and then the Waffen-SS would return to its original role of a State Police Force, so he did not consider it worth upsetting the generals by 'raising up the spectre of a party army'. So Himmler in his capacity as *Reichsführer* and Chief of the German Police transferred enough men from the SS Death's Head regiments, who guarded the concentration camps, and the German police to form two new divisions. He then replaced these men by a new intake of volunteers who were not subject to military conscription. This enabled Himmler to enlarge the *Leibstandarte SS Adolf Hitler* to a reinforced motorized infantry regiment and form the three pre-war SS-VT regiments into a division, which was at first called the *SS-Verfügungs-Division* and later *Das Reich*. The Death's Head personnel were assembled at Dachau concentration camp, which had been cleared of inmates, and formed into another division (*SS-Totenkopf-Division*) and finally a large number of police reservists were organized into the *Polizei-Division* (later *SS-Polizei-Division*). The intake of thousands of reservists who were neither SS men nor National Socialists was a considerable dilution of the SS elite status, but there was yet another influx of outsiders into these early Waffen-SS divisions. These were the specialists and technicians from the German Army who were transferred to the Waffen-SS to provide the essential divisional artillery and ancillary units. By the end of November 1939 Himmler's army consisted of a motorized regiment, three divisions, fourteen Death's Head regiments and two officer cadet academies as well as a number of ancillary units and establishments.

For the purpose of studying the degree of criminality of the Waffen-SS, it is necessary to describe in detail the complex origins of the *SS-Totenkopfverbände* (SS Death's Head units) and what became in effect the second Waffen-SS. Many historians consider that it was the influx of the Death's Head personnel from the concentration camps, that led the Waffen-SS to commit more atrocities than any other branch of the German armed forces but this is a gross over-simplification.

As early as 1934 it had been envisaged that in an emergency 25,000 *Allgemeine-SS* men could be used to reinforce the Political Police, rather than be called up for military service.

By 1935 these men were being referred to as Police Reinforcements/*SS Guard Formations* (*Polizeiverstärkung* (*SS-Wachverbände*)) which suggests that it was intended that the concentration camp guard units would be used to help put down civil disorders.

By 1938 two special training units had been formed, and from the concentration camp guards, *Allgemeine-SS* men, ethnic Germans, SA and NSKK (National Socialist Transport Corps) men and youths too young for military service, sufficient personnel (33,000 by June 1940) had been produced to form the *SS-Totenkopf-Division*, and fifteen *SS-Totenkopf-Standarten* (regiments) together with their replacement units. Following the German defeat of Poland some of these Death's Head regiments were used as garrison troops, and became involved in the ruthless subjugation of the Polish people in which hundreds of thousands were arbitrarily executed. So disgusted were some of the senior Army commanders at the excesses committed by the SS, that they not only court-martialled individual SS men, but registered their displeasure at the fact that the SS Death's Head troopers were wearing the field-grey uniform of the German Army although they did not form part of the armed forces. The SS reply was that these SS troops had been 'committed to special military duties by the *Führer*', and anyway it was too late to change the uniform.

The final stage in the development of this second Waffen-SS began in August 1940, following the German victory in the West. The Inspectorate of SS Death's Head Regiments was dissolved and the command of these police troops was transferred to the headquarters of the Waffen-SS proper. Himmler was always on the look-out for ways to increase the Waffen-SS and thereby his own prestige within the Nazi hierarchy. Experience in Poland had shown that many of the routine tasks assigned to the Death's Head regiments could be carried out by the German police, which also possessed militarily organized armed battalions. But the only way Himmler could get the Army to recognize the Death's Head regiments as part of the armed forces was to relinquish control over them, and this he was always loath to do. Eventually a compromise solution was worked out, and in March 1941 nine Death's Head infantry and two cavalry regiments were redesignated SS Infantry and Cavalry regiments. Three Death's Head Infantry regiments were formed into a Waffen-SS Battle Group (*SS-Kampfgruppe Nord*), and one regiment was transferred to the Waffen-SS Motorized Division *Reich* (later *Das Reich*). The remaining five infantry and two cavalry regiments were placed under the command of a newly created staff called *Kommandostab Reichsführer-SS*. Himmler retained control over this formation and used it for 'special assignments' in the rear, but the German Army could also call upon the staff to carry out operations in support of the Armed Forces directly behind the front line. Ostensibly this second Waffen-SS was engaged in fighting partisans, and this was a convenient cloak under which the SS could cleanse the occupied Eastern territories of all political, intellectual and racial enemies.

In recent years Waffen-SS apologists have changed their tune. Under the weight of documentary evidence they have given up trying to disassociate the Waffen-SS from the activities of the concentration camps and special action groups (*Einsatzgruppen*) per se. They now make a distinction between the regular or 'Front' Waffen-SS which served almost continuously under Army command at the front, and so could not have had anything to do with the massacre of the civilians behind the front, and the Waffen-SS as a whole. As we have seen the Waffen-SS men who provided the firing squads for the *Einsatzkommando* massacres came in the main from those Waffen-SS units which remained under Himmler's exclusive command.

Back now to the Waffen-SS proper.

The German Army which imposed such a crushing defeat on Holland, Belgium and France in 1940 was composed of one hundred and forty divisions while the Waffen-SS contributed three divisions and a reinforced regiment. This was not a significant contribution, but the infantry divisions of the Waffen-SS were motorized, and in that respect they represented a high percentage of the infantry divisions capable of keeping up with the fast-moving armoured divisions. Always in the vanguard the Waffen-SS suffered heavy losses but gained invaluable experience, and finally won for itself – at Hitler's behest – more than its share of the victor's accolade, and the term Waffen-SS became indelibly etched on the minds of the German public.

The invasions of Yugoslavia and Greece were annoying distractions for Hitler who was in the midst of planning his greatest undertaking – the invasion of the Soviet Union. However, it gave the Waffen-SS another opportunity to demonstrate its new-found confidence in its military prowess.

The military phase would be carried out by the Wehrmacht and its allies and the divisions of the Waffen-SS, which now numbered one hundred and sixty thousand men. The subjugation of the civil population in the occupied territories and the programme of colonization would be planned and executed by the SS. Security would be the responsibility of Reinhard Heydrich's Security Police and the Special Action Groups (*Einsatzgruppen*) and the ordinary German Police. The vast reshuffling of the civilian population in the newly conquered areas would be the responsibility of Walther Darré's SS Race and Resettlement Office.

For Operation Barbarossa the four divisions of the Waffen-SS were distributed amongst the three German Army Groups. In reserve in the north, facing the Baltic countries and Leningrad, were the *SS-Totenkopf* and *SS-Polizei* divisions. In Army Group Centre, poised at Moscow, was *SS-Division Reich*, while in Army Group South were the *Leibstandarte SS Adolf Hitler* and *SS-Division Wiking*. This last-named division with its large proportion of volunteers from the 'Germanic' countries was to make the deepest penetration into Soviet territory. In the far north were the

SS-Kampfgruppe Nord and SS Infantry Regiment 9. Immediately behind Army Group Centre was the Commando Staff RFSS with its SS infantry and cavalry brigades. Their task was to mop up the pockets of Red Army soldiers who had been cut off and by-passed by the advancing German armoured formations.

In the years preceding the German invasion, the Soviet people were just beginning to recover from the deprivations caused by World War I, the Revolution, Civil War and collectivization which had decimated the population and caused widespread famine. As the mechanized units of the German Wehrmacht poured into the Ukraine and White Russia they were often hailed as liberators.

Since it is in the interests of fighting troops to leave behind them a friendly or at least passive civil population as they advance into enemy territory, contacts between the Waffen-SS troops and the civil population were brief and on the whole correct. There were a few cases of rape reported but no widespread looting, pillage or murder. But following closely behind were other SS units whose personnel wore the same field-grey uniform. Their task was to ensure order and security in the rear areas, but their principal achievement was to antagonize the civil population, and create the ideal conditions for the creation of an armed resistance to the Fascist invaders.

Former Waffen-SS men point out that since the field formations of the Waffen-SS were under Army command they could only carry out Army orders, and were thus not in a position to execute orders of a political nature. However they do not deny that the war in the Soviet Union was governed by a completely different code of conduct to that which existed during the campaigns in Western Europe. In part this was due to the Soviet Union refusing to become a signatory to the Geneva Convention, but principally it was the result of the brutalizing effect of Nazi '*Untermensch*' (sub-human) propaganda which equated bolshevism with Jewry and both with oriental bestiality. This was confirmed in the eyes of the average SS soldier, by the primitive conditions which he encountered in towns and villages in the Soviet Union. The masses of Red Army soldiers captured by the Germans in the opening months of the campaign were simply herded together and left in the open to starve. The sight of emaciated and dirty Soviet soldiers grovelling in the dust for a scrap of bread did not always arouse sympathy in the German soldier, but encouraged him to treat Russians as sub-humans.

Almost immediately the Soviets recognized that the soldiers with the death's head emblem on their caps were a particularly tough and ruthless branch of the German Armed Forces, and by the first winter of the war on the eastern front, the shooting of SS prisoners was widespread. Hans Wissebach fought with the *SS-Totenkopf-Division* at Biakovo in the Demjansk Pocket. In March 1942, with the temperature at 35 degrees below freezing, Wissebach was blown-up and blinded. He remembers lying in a trench with five wounded comrades when the Russians came and shot four of the six SS men. Wissebach reckons he was spared because he was an officer. When he eventually returned to West Germany twelve years later, Wissebach learnt that he was probably the only Waffen-SS officer taken prisoner in the first year of fighting on the eastern front, to have survived. But there is much documentary proof that the shooting of prisoners of war and brutality on both sides was widespread. After the war the Soviet authorities accused the Waffen-SS of terrible crimes against Red Army personnel and Soviet citizens, but little documentary evidence was forthcoming, and Soviet prosecutors at the Nuremberg trials did not press charges, since they probably feared that a detailed investigation by an international court of events in the war zone would also expose Soviet callousness and indifference to the suffering of its *own* population.

When the Soviet winter offensive ground to a halt at the beginning of 1942, the field formations of the Waffen-SS were mere shadows of their former selves. But in those terrible defensive battles the Waffen-SS came of age and showed that not only in attack was it a formidable force, but that also in defeat it never lost its spirit. Even after the failure of the first phase of the invasion of the Soviet Union, Hitler was convinced that victory was near at hand, and so for the time being he resisted Himmler's appeals for an unlimited expansion of the Waffen-SS.

After rest and refitting in France and Belgium the three divisions – *Leibstandarte SS Adolf Hitler*, *Das Reich* and *Totenkopf*, now equipped with a tank component and designated as Panzer Grenadier divisions, returned once again to Russia to join the rest of the Waffen-SS on the eastern front. Waffen-SS order of battle now stood at six divisions, two infantry and one cavalry brigades, four legions of foreign volunteers and a few independent units. In the summer of 1942 the Waffen-SS was heavily engaged in the summer counter-offensive in the Kursk area, and as the Axis forces surged into the Caucasus, it was the pan-Germanic *SS-Division Wiking* which made the deepest penetration into the Soviet hinterland.

The war on the eastern front had reached a far too critical stage for it to remain simply a proving ground for a future German police force, and Hitler decided the time had now come for the maximum exploitation of the remarkable fighting qualities of the Waffen-SS. From a fighting strength in September 1942 of 142,000 the Waffen-SS doubled its strength in 1943. That year the Waffen-SS was transformed into a formidable armoured force of seven Panzer divisions all of which began to receive lavish quantities of the very latest equipment. Hitler also saw that Army restrictions on SS recruitment were lifted, and the SS was able to get all the men it needed. But there was no longer a steady stream of bright-eyed youths eagerly seeking glory in the victorious and invincible Waffen-SS. Now everyone could see that the war was turning irrevocably against Germany, and the German public were becoming increasingly aware of the extent of the losses on the eastern front (over a million by February

1942), particularly in the Waffen-SS which was always in the forefront of the fighting. The pre-war cadre of hand-picked SS volunteers which had created this remarkable fighting machine had been decimated, and now Himmler had no choice but to accept experienced commanders from the Army and conscript the rank and file for his new armoured divisions. These conscripts were not very happy to be called up, and even less happy at finding themselves in the Waffen-SS. Nevertheless, the Waffen-SS spirit transferred itself to these new SS Panzer divisions, which despite the different character of the personnel – now really indistinguishable from that found in the German Army – became every bit as formidable and dangerous as the original divisions of the Waffen-SS.

Now that he had permitted the creation of an elite armoured force of considerable strength, Hitler tried to keep it in reserve for use in special emergencies. Such a moment developed in the late summer and autumn of 1943. With the situation on the eastern front still dangerous, Hitler withdrew an SS Panzer Corps, and sent it to Italy to prevent the country falling into the lap of the Allies. The commander of Army Group Centre, Field-Marshal von Kluge, protested vehemently, but Hitler was adamant 'down there I can only accomplish something with elite formations which are close to Fascism'.

While the *SS-Totenkopf* and *Wiking* divisions remained in Russia, the *Leibstandarte* moved to the West where it remained until December 1943, before returning once again to the eastern front. During its sojourn in Italy it helped disarm the Italian Army and became embroiled in what to all intents and purposes was rapidly becoming a civil war in Italy. While operating against anti-Fascist partisans the *Leibstandarte* was accused of razing to the ground the northern Italian town of Boves, and killing many of its inhabitants as a reprisal.

Das Reich left Russia in April 1944 for rest and refitting in southern France. In an operation against the Maquis in the Auvergne, SS troops found the bodies of sixty German soldiers in the village of Tulle. SS reaction was rapid and violent and ninety-one men and women were strung up from lamp-posts. In June 1944 *Das Reich* was ordered north to Normandy to help repel the Allied invasion. The journey northwards through the countryside infested with partisans was tense and dangerous. After many frustrating delays one of the division's officers was shot by a sniper near the town of Oradour sur Glane. Men of the 4th Panzer Grenadier Regiment *Der Führer* (originally formed from Austrians but by now containing a large number of Alsacians*) descended on the village, herded all the inhabitants into the church, and burned it down on top of them. Six hundred and forty-two adults and two hundred and seven children died as a result of this outrage.

In the bitter fighting which developed in Normandy between the Allies trying to break out of their beach-head and the Germans who were trying to drive them back into the sea, the Waffen-SS was heavily involved. The 1st SS Panzer Corps with the divisions *Leibstandarte*, *Das Reich*, and a newly formed division of eighteen-year-old Hitler Youths fought desperately and with great skill, despite being blasted by heavy naval artillery and overwhelming Allied air superiority. Particularly vicious were the scraps which developed between the 12 SS Panzer Division *Hitler-Jugend* and the Canadians and 1st Polish Armoured Division. The Canadians and Poles found themselves facing a tough and ruthless foe and the Poles often found themselves being fired upon from behind by stay-behind teams of baby-faced Hitler Youths in camouflage uniforms and thereafter shot many of their prisoners. The Hitler Youth Division was also accused by the Canadians of shooting their prisoners. After the war the thirty-five-year-old *SS-Brigadeführer* (Major-General) Kurt Meyer, one of the youngest generals in the German

* Ironically at the trial held in Bordeaux a number of Alsacian defendants who had been conscripted into the Waffen-SS had, in the meantime, served with distinction in the French Army in Indo-China where some of them had been decorated.

armed forces, was put on trial in Canada for the activities of his division in Normandy.

Despite the arrival at the end of June 1944 of the 2nd SS Panzer Corps, with the newly formed 9th and 10th SS Panzer Divisions, the Allies succeeded in breaking out of their bridgehead by the end of July and despite Waffen-SS efforts the battle of Normandy was lost. The SS Panzer Corps remained in the West for the rest of 1944, and took part in Hitler's final offensive in the Ardennes in December, before returning for the last time to the eastern front, which now passed through Hungary.

It was during this last offensive in the West that the Waffen-SS is supposed to have committed yet another war crime. A battle group commanded by Joachim Peiper from the 1st Panzer Division *Leibstandarte SS Adolf Hitler* shot seventy-one American soldiers who had just surrendered near Malmedy in the Ardennes.

This crime was significant because it was the only large massacre of American soldiers, and had much to do with American insistence that the SS be declared a criminal organization at the Nuremberg trials.

After the war a large number of Waffen-SS soldiers were put on trial, and although sentenced to long terms of imprisonment or death, only one death sentence – that of Fritz Knochlein – found guilty by a British military court of massacring British prisoners of war in Flanders in May 1940 – was carried out. Ten years after the war all but one Waffen-SS man had been released. But today, thirty-six years after the end of the war, an Austrian, Walther Reder, is still being held by the Italian authorities in a military prison in Gaeta.

Only in the massacre of Canadian and British prisoners of war in Normandy was there any evidence to suggest that the shooting of prisoners of war by Waffen-SS units formed part of official SS policy, or had been ordered by a senior commander. In all known cases – Le Paradis, Boves, Marzabotto, Tulle, Oradour sur Glane, Klissura, Oradour and Malmedy – brutal reprisals were ordered by junior officers, either in the heat of battle or in furious revenge for what they saw as underhand acts of murder by non-uniformed *Franc-tireurs* against regular soldiers.

In the immediate postwar period with emotions running high it was, and still is, difficult to see the crimes committed by the Waffen-SS as distinct from those committed by the SS as a whole. During World War II the Allied armies had never had to contend with a hostile population, nor were they subjected to surprise attack and ambush by partisans in their rear, but in the postwar period it was a different story. The French experienced Indo-China and Algeria, the British, Palestine, Malaya, Kenya, Aden and Cyprus and currently Northern Ireland, and of course America went through the traumatic experience in Vietnam. In all these wars young soldiers – mostly conscripts – found themselves in the role of occupiers and oppressors and when fired upon and murdered by terrorists (or freedom fighters depending on your point of view) they too had to resort to rounding up civilians, women and children included, burning down villages, and extracting information from suspects by the use of torture. Even with restraints imposed upon them by democratic governments and with the press never far away, atrocities were also committed.

Richard Schulze-Kossens' statement about Waffen-SS war crimes might equally apply to Lieutenant William Calley, the young American officer accused of wiping out the Vietnamese village of Mi Lai:

'Let me say as a soldier I condemn all crimes regardless of who committed them, whether by us or by others, and that includes the crimes committed against captured SS men after the capitulation. But I make no reproaches in that respect. I am not recriminating, I only want to say that in war, amongst the mass of soldiers, there are always elements who develop criminal tendencies, and I can only condemn them. I would not say that the Waffen-SS was typically criminal, but there are well-known incidents. I don't want to excuse anything, but I must say one thing which is, that it is natural in war,

during hot and heavy fighting, for young officers to sometimes lose their nerve. I want to mention one example of this,
Tulle in France, where a company found the bodies of sixty
German soldiers who had not been killed in action but murdered. There they lie wounded and mutilated, and then in an
instant there is a desire for revenge and they lose their nerve.
But if I have to mention other crimes – war crimes, then let
me mention Oradour. The Division in question had seventy
companies and, because of partisans, one company often
found itself fighting civilians and got into a situation which
would have led to the commander being court-martialled,
had he not been killed in action. I am not excusing this at all,
and anyway nothing can be done about it, only war does
generate inhuman impulses which might overwhelm someone who carries too great a responsibility at too young an
age.'

The Final Solution 1933–1945

*Today I will be a prophet once again. If the
international Jewish financiers inside and
outside Europe should again succeed in
plunging the nations into a world war, the
result will not be the bolshevization of the earth
and thereby the victory of Jewry, but the
annihilation of the Jewish race in Europe.*

ADOLF HITLER
30 January 1939

Gerald Reitlinger in his definitive history of the Final Solution described the Nazi seizure of power as 'a revolution with no dispossessed class'. The socialist content of National Socialism was real enough to satisfy most former socialists and even some Communists. Hitler immediately reassured the capitalists and industrialists that they had a vital role to play in the new nationalist era, and that they had nothing to fear from the increase of socialism. The established churches were not interfered with and paradoxically the one element in German society which refused to settle down was within the Nazi Party itself. The moment Hitler came to power the whole *raison d'être* of the fighting formations of the Nazi Party – the brown-shirted SA and even the SS – was at an end. Street fighting and pub brawling were things of the past, while provocative marches with beating drums and waving banners no longer had any point. Despite Hitler's warnings that the revolution was over and an immediate return to normality was essential if Germany was to recover her lost power and prosperity, the radical elements in his party saw the seizure of power as just a beginning. It took the ruthless emasculation of the SA by the SS to finally bring SA revolutionary aspirations to an end, and allow the era of the SS to begin.

As early as 1930 Himmler had foreseen the main role of the SS to be of a police nature and by taking over first the political police and then the whole German police, Himmler switched the political struggle from the streets to the police stations, courts and concentration camps and all aspects of anti-Nazism – both ideological and racial – were gradually covered by appropriate National Socialist legislation. The SS assured its continued existence by becoming a sort of ideological watchdog. However, the most peculiar achievement was to remove the last remaining target for the brutal energies of the frustrated 'old party fighters' – the Jews. Anti-semitism in Nazi Germany came in waves and was neither spontaneous nor particularly popular. Within the Nazi Party leading factions emerged which saw the 'Jewish problem' as a question of race (the SS), in economic terms (Göring) or as a sort of Jew-baiting distraction for the embittered proletariat (Julius Streicher and later Josef Goebbels). But nowhere amongst this diversity of opinion was there any indication that the final solution would be extermination.

There had been bloody anti-Jewish pogroms in Germany when Hitler came to power in March 1933, and these were followed by a boycott of Jewish businesses and widespread dismissals of Jews from the government and professions which led to the first mass exodus of Jews. In 1934 things seemed to have returned to normal and ten thousand Jews returned to Germany, but in 1935 further anti-Jewish measures were introduced and 'Jews not wanted' signs appeared. All these measures were inspired by Julius Streicher, *Gauleiter* of Franconia and publisher of the pornographic anti-Semitic newspaper *Der Stürmer* and the Reich Minister for the People's Enlightenment, Dr Josef Goebbels, and were disapproved of by the 'better sort of people' in the SS – or rather SD – who were trying to find a lasting solution in a cold and rational way.

On 15 September 1935 two new laws were passed – the Reich Law of Citizenship and the Law for the Protection of German Blood and Honour. They were publicly unveiled at the 1935 Nazi Party Congress (Party Day of Freedom) and became known as the Nuremberg Laws. Reitlinger described them as 'the most murderous legislative instrument known to European history'. These laws and their thirteen supplementary decrees were progressively to remove Jews from the protection of the law, while at the same time creating the legal framework for their dispossession and banishment. The long-term aim of this legislation was to make Germany Jew-free.

Despite the combination of legislative vindictiveness and ever-increasing incidents of crude petty humiliations, Germany's 503,000 Jews showed a marked reluctance to leave their homeland, and it became necessary for the SD to set up a special office for Jewish emigration which carried on a bizarre association with German Zionist organizations. Both the SD and the Zionists were anxious to promote Jewish emigration to Palestine.

The organizer of the Central Office for Jewish Emigration from August 1938 was Adolf Eichmann who acted with increasing urgency until the term emigration became synonymous with deportation. This policy could only continue successfully as long as Germany's frontiers remained open and foreign countries accepted Jewish emigrées. But a squabble developed between Germany and Poland over the question of sixty thousand Polish Jews resident in Germany. In October 1938, seventeen thousand of them were driven across the German frontier into Poland under conditions of great hardship. Amongst the Jews was a tailor from Hanover called Grynszpan and when his son in Paris heard about the way in which his father had been treated, he tried to shoot the German ambassador, but instead shot and fatally wounded a junior official in the German Embassy in Paris. The resulting outcry in Germany was carefully orchestrated by Josef Goebbels and developed into Germany's first official pogrom or, as it became known, 'plate glass night' (*Kristallnacht*). The SS was taken by surprise and the first SD chief Reinhard Heydrich knew about the disturbances was the sight of a burning synagogue in the centre of Munich. SS units were confined to barracks and SS men were ordered not to participate in the pogrom, while all SD and Gestapo personnel were to do was to secure Jewish property. Heydrich's report to Göring on the 11 November 1938 listed one hundred and ninety-one synagogues burnt, and seven thousand five hundred shops looted. Thirty-six Jews were killed and twenty thousand Jews were sent to concentration camps 'for their own protection'.

Time was rapidly running out for the Jews of Germany and the newly acquired territories of Austria and Czechoslovakia. Life was becoming increasingly intolerable as anti-Jewish legislation multiplied, and the Aryan populations became increasingly influenced by anti-Jewish propaganda. Emigration went on apace until one month before the German invasion of Poland in September 1939. It was now time to implement the second part of Hitler's prophesy, but it took him another two years before he finally ordered the physical extermination of the Jews.

Heydrich's SD and Gestapo *Einsatzgruppen* followed closely behind the advancing German armies into Poland. Their primary target was not so much Poland's huge Jewish population – just under three and a half million in 1939 – but the elements of Polish society which could pose the greatest threat to Germany's despotism. There were, of course, many outrages committed against Jews by individual SS men and even German military personnel, but in October, Jews resident in the territories incorporated in the Reich, like Bromberg, began to be systematically massacred. On 21 September 1939 Heydrich ordered his *Einsatzgruppen* to remove all Jews from rural areas and concentrate them in towns prior to their deportation eastwards to those parts of Poland now designated the Government General by the Germans. These first mass deportations were organized by none other than *SS-Hauptsturmführer* (Captain) Adolf Eichmann. Eichmann was fast becoming a key figure in the final solution. Although not very intelligent he had a genius for organization, and at a time when it was difficult to cope with the transportation system he was able to get out of Germany those Jews who wanted to emigrate, thus in a way saving their lives. Later when the demand on Germany's overstretched railway system was even greater, Eichmann was equally successful in getting his victims to the extermination camps.

Between the end of the Polish campaign and the invasion of the Soviet Union all parties involved in the Jewish question still considered emigration as the only solution, but now that Britain and Germany were at war Palestine was out of the question. The idea of a Jewish state in Poland offended the tidy German mind because it was not a final solution, and such a state would be difficult to isolate. The other serious contender was Madagascar; the idea of an island ghetto for four million Jews in the middle of the Indian Ocean was received with great enthusiasm in the SD. With typical German thoroughness everything was planned down to the last detail, and German Jews were even deported to France on the first leg of their journey there, when suddenly the whole project was dropped. Instead Jews from all over Europe were packed into ghettos in Lodz, Warsaw, Cracow, Lublin, Radom, Lemberg, as well as in many smaller towns. The ancient fabric of these ghettos collapsed under the weight of so much humanity and overcrowding, lack of sanitation and malnutrition led to an appalling death rate. It is estimated that at least five hundred thousand Jews died in the Polish ghettos and labour camps.

Sometime during the detailed planning of the invasion of the Soviet Union – probably while drafting the notorious order to shoot Soviet political commissars – Hitler gave the verbal order for the physical extermination of the Jews. The first steps in this horrendous undertaking were carried out by Heydrich's *Einsatzgruppen*, which by November 1941 had already accounted for at least one million victims, although not all of them were Jews. The four thousand men of the *Einsatzgruppen* were drawn from the Gestapo, SD, German police and from the Waffen-SS, but even with the continued co-operation of pro-German, or rather anti-Bolshevik, locally raised militias, it was obvious that a force of this size couldn't possibly cope with the enormity of the task ahead. Added to this was the fact that the brutal and indiscriminate murder of the intelligentsia, clergy, Jews, gypsies, including large numbers of women and children, often in public, was driving people into the arms of the partisans. The failure of the Germans to carry with it the popular support which it had often encountered in the territories liberated from Stalinist terror was disastrous. But to Hitler it 'was not without its advantages as far as we are concerned because it gives us the chance to wipe out anyone who gets in our way'.

Despite the scale of *Einsatzgruppen* successes, there still remained vast numbers of Jews in ghettos and labour camps in Poland and the occupied eastern territories, as well as the Jewish populations of western and south-eastern Europe, and it was obvious that the final solution could only become a reality if it became a separate undertaking. On 20 January 1942 a conference was held at Wansee near Berlin at which all agencies involved in the Jewish question – the SD, the Führer and party chancelleries, the Ministries of the Interior, Justice and Foreign Affairs, the Four Year Plan and the Reich Ministry for the Occupied Eastern Territories. It was chaired by Reinhard Heydrich and the minutes were kept by Adolf Eichmann.

Senior Chief Public Prosecutor Alfred Spiess the Federal German Republic's leading expert on 'Operation Reinhard'* takes up the story: 'Hitler gave the order for the killing of the Jews to Himmler as Reich Leader of the SS and Chief of the German Police, who in turn passed it on to Reinhard Heydrich, Chief of the Security Police. The organizational machinery for the rounding up and transportation of the Jews was set up in the Reich Security Headquarters in Department 4B4 – often referred to as the Jewish Department. In the

* The cover name for the 31 July 1941 order empowering Reinhard Heydrich with the planning and implementation of the 'final solution of the Jewish problem'.

Government General (Poland), *SS-Gruppenführer* Odilo Globocnik – former *Gauleiter* of Vienna – was made responsible for overseeing the exterminations. He had constructed three extermination camps on the banks of the river Bug at Treblinka, Sobibor and Belszec. First and foremost these camps were to dispose of the Jews of eastern Europe, but once they had all been killed and the camps cleared, transports began to arrive from western and south-western Europe.'

A question of great interest is where did the personnel who organized and ran these camps come from? In 1939 just before the beginning of the war, Hitler gave the order to begin a Euthanasia Programme, and it happens that a copy of this written order to Reichsleiter Philip Bouhler (head of Hitler's chancellery and honorary *SS-Obergruppenführer* (General)) has survived, whereas Hitler never gave a written order, only a verbal one, for the extermination of the Jews. The headquarters of the Euthanasia Programme was at Tiergartenstrasse 4 in Berlin-Charlottenburg, and the people who were involved in this programme became known as the T4 people. They came from a variety of professions, and had quite possibly reported for duty at some completely different department. For example there was a medical orderly sergeant in the Treblinka Trial* who was ordered to report to T4 because he was a medical orderly. Another was a male nurse from a mental hospital who was recruited by T4 because he had worked with the mentally sick. There was also a dairy worker who reported for duty with the police and was told there was another post in a mental hospital, and before he knew it he was in T4, and so in the course of time a group of personnel was assembled who killed mental patients under the auspices of T4.

The exact procedure by which personnel were selected for the Euthanasia Programme is not known, but research suggests that the administrative posts were filled by people who

---

* The trial held in Dusseldorf in 1970 which ended with the commandant of the camp in which it is estimated that 900,000 people met their death – Franz Stangl – being sentenced to life imprisonment.

had heard from friends about what they thought was a cushy job in the *Führer*'s chancellory and applied without knowing exactly what the job entailed. Those who carried out the actual killings and other menial jobs came mostly from the German police in Stuttgart and Linz in Austria, and they were picked out by some sergeant on the basis of 'you, you and you'. To impress upon all these people both the 'legality' and secrecy of their work, about which they still knew nothing, each newcomer, 'even the chars', was personally interviewed by Reichsleiter Bouhler's deputy *SS-Oberführer* (Brigadier) Victor Brack.

In a number of mental institutions – about twelve in all – small gas chambers were constructed in which the incurably sick could be gassed. The staff of these institutions consisted of both male and female doctors who were responsible for the inspection of those who were to be killed and all medical matters, police officials to ensure the correct running of the institution and the issuance of falsified death certificates, and finally the men known as 'burners' who carried out the gassings. Strange as it may seem there was hardly an SS uniform to be seen because the staff wore either plain clothes, or, if policemen, the green uniform of the German police. The man responsible for carrying out the very first gassings was the Württemberg police official Christian 'savage Christian' Wirth. By mid-1940 Wirth had become a sort of roving inspector of killing institutions and Germany's first gassing expert.

Despite the secrecy of the Euthanasia Programme it had become common knowledge by May 1941 and by October had virtually ceased. It has long been thought that Hitler was taken by surprise at the degree of public indignation at the mercy killings, particularly from the Catholic Church, that he bowed to public opinion and halted the programme. It is also probable that Hitler only intended the programme to last for about half a year by which time all those who were to be killed were already dead. The truth is that the programme did not come to an end, but simply switched its targets. In

November 1941, the Charitable Foundation for Institutional Care (official cover name for T4) transferred its activities from the mental homes to the concentration camps. The names of concentration camp inmates considered by the commandant to be habitual criminals, perverts, or simple-minded were inspected by a medical commission and entered on falsified lunacy certificates which bore the number 14F13. They were then despatched to the euthanasia centres and killed. The new twist was that included in this category of people were large numbers of political prisoners and Jews. The existing institutional gas chambers which could only deal with a maximum of one hundred victims at a time couldn't cope with the steady stream of blacked-out coaches which arrived night after night. The inability of existing facilities to deal with the 14F13 killings was to lead to the construction of gas chambers in German concentration camps.

In August 1941 the initial wave of euthanasia killings had come to an end, and when by October the winding-up procedure had been completed there was nothing more for the T4 people to do. The 14F13 killings did not require the services of these specialists. Meanwhile on the eastern front the Soviet winter offensive had driven back the German forces with heavy losses, while the lack of adequate winter clothing in such a bitter winter had caused terrible suffering from exposure and frost-bite. At short notice about four hundred T4 people had been formed into a Waffen-SS medical unit and rushed to the eastern front, but each man carried in his paybook a slip of red paper issued by the Army High Command which prevented a T4 man being sent to the front line where he stood the risk of being taken prisoner by the Soviets.

Meanwhile other T4 personnel had been sent to Poland where a euthanasia centre had been established in an old castle at Chelmno (Kulmhof in German) where Christian Wirth had been experimenting with a van into which victims were enticed or forced, and then gassed by exhaust fumes as they were driven to burial pits in nearby woods. The gas vans were not reliable and in due course were replaced by gas chambers in which Poles suffering from tuberculosis were killed. When at the beginning of 1942 'Operation Reinhard' began, it was decided to establish three extermination camps at Belsec, Sobibor and Treblinka in eastern Poland, where the ideal conditions of isolation and good railway communications had been found for the secret mass-gassing of Europe's Jewish population.

The ninety-six T4 people who were chosen to operate these centres had been selected on the basis of their past record while working in the German euthanasia centres, and mostly came from the General SS (*Allgemeine-SS*) but also included SD, Waffen-SS men and German policemen, mostly with non-commissioned officer or junior officer rank. In each of the three camps there was a guard unit of about one hundred Ukrainian auxiliaries, and a special Jewish commando of between seven hundred and one thousand selected 'work' Jews, who in order to save their lives helped in the extermination of their brethren. These camps existed for about seventeen months and during this very limited time span about one hundred Germans and a few auxiliaries accounted for over two million Jews and gypsies. A truly staggering ratio.

The awareness of exactly what was going on in these extermination camps came gradually even to those involved in the operation. Having decided at Wansee to implement the Final Solution nobody was very anxious to discuss how it was to be done. The practical details were left to Odilo Globocnik who entrusted the task to Wirth. Bouhler as head of T4 assigned his specialists to Globocnik without, as he claimed after the war, any idea that they were to murder Jews, until Globocnik actually told him in June 1942. Apparently Bouhler did know because he was anxious about the psychological effect this work would have on his men because there was a lot of difference between the mercy killing of the incurably sick and the cold-blooded murder of perfectly healthy men, women and children. For this reason the T4 people did not discover the exact nature of their work until they arrived at the camps and found out for themselves, but then it was almost too late to back out. The reaction of Franz Stangl, commandant of Sobibor, on discovering that he had been posted to an extermination camp was typical: 'I simply wasn't up to such an assignment and contemplated deserting.' But he found that 'at Sobibor one could avoid seeing almost all of it' (extermination process) so he stayed. A Waffen-SS man arrived at Treblinka after being transferred from the front and when he discovered what was going on he said to the commandant 'what's going on here is a *schweinerei* [literally dirty business] and I will not lend my hand to it'. Half an hour later he had received his marching orders and rejoined his unit. Others identified themselves in varying degrees with the murderous policies of the Nazi State and took full advantage of the privileges accorded them: more leave, no danger of being sent to the front, use of a special T4 rest home, and plenty of food and drink, and the opportunity of helping themselves to the many valuables taken from their victims. In fact alcohol played an important part in the off-duty life of both the Germans and their auxiliaries. It acted not only as a tranquillizer for those with troubled souls, but as a stimulant for the majority who became increasingly demoralized. Alfred Spiess tells the following story which is a graphic illustration of the atmosphere in Treblinka:

'There is evidence that the murder of the first hundred thousand Jews from Warsaw was celebrated. Naturally, the conversation in the canteen in the evenings got round to what was going on. There was an SS man – who was later acquitted – who was sitting in the canteen with a group drinking beer and wine, and said, "What we're doing here is a disgusting business, it's a hideous crime that will catch up with us one day. One day we'll have to answer for it." This SS man was threatened with a beating by the others and even felt his life in danger because of what he had said.'

This chapter is nearly at an end and yet there is no mention of probably the best known of all camps – Auschwitz. Ausch-witz and another camp in Lublin called Majdanek were typical examples of the blurring of lines of demarcation between one branch of the SS and another. Whereas the extermination camps had been run by the Security Police, Auschwitz and Majdanek were technically Waffen-SS concentration camps run by the SS Economic and Administrative Office. But in September 1941 gassings of the camp's sick began to be carried out at Auschwitz on a limited scale, and following Himmler's visit in July 1942, during which he had called for and silently watched a demonstration extermination of a transport of Jews, Auschwitz/Birkenau became the largest extermination camp of all, in which it is estimated at least seven hundred and fifty thousand died by gassing, injection and other causes.

Majdanek was created as a result of Himmler's visit to Globocnik in July 1941 and was originally conceived as a labour camp for Soviet prisoners of war and Jews, and as an SS settlement. Its contribution to the Final Solution was at least two hundred and fifty thousand victims. These two camps became pawns in a struggle between those final solution fanatics who wanted to kill every Jew they could lay their hands on, and those who wanted to exploit the potential of Jewish labour until the war was won, and then deal with them. As long as Jews continued to be employed in SS industries they had a chance of survival.

The final chapter in this horrendous story is the story of the closing down of the extermination camps and the removal of every trace of their existence by a special SS Commando 1005. Buildings were demolished, putrifying corpses exhumed and burnt on pyres made from railway lines or in trenches filled with petrol, the ground ploughed over and trees planted. The T4 personnel were transferred to Trieste where a particularly savage war against Yugoslav partisans was in progress, and where it was hoped that men who had become an embarrassment in defeat might find a convenient death.

The Reckoning

*Whatever happens do not let us depart from
the principle that war criminals shall be dealt
with because they are proved to be criminals
and not because they belong to a race led by a
maniac and a murderer who has brought this
frightful evil upon the World.*

HANSARD
December 1943

By the spring of 1942 the Allies had a pretty good idea of
what was going on in Germany and the occupied eastern
territories. Information had leaked out via neutral sources
such as the Vatican and the various resistance movements,
that terrible crimes were being committed by the SS against
the incurably sick, the clergy, political opponents of Nazism,
intellectuals, Slavs, Jews and gypsies, but it was not until the
last months of the war that camps like Belsen, Buchenwald
and Dachau were liberated by the Allies and the full extent
and scale of the horrors became known throughout the world.
The fact that even more terrible camps had existed on Polish
soil during the dark years of the German occupation took
longer to percolate through to the West.

As soon as Allied troops landed in Normandy on 6 June
1944, they began to experience the toughness and determination of their Waffen-SS opponents. According to the Allied
Supreme Commander General Eisenhower: 'SS morale
backed by blind confidence in ultimate Nazi victory, was
extremely good, and whether in attack or defence they fought
to a man with fanatical courage.' But that fanatical courage
was also tinged with a ruthlessness which seemed to set the
Waffen-SS apart from the rest of the German armed forces,

and the Allied armies in western Europe began to experience incidents of 'unsoldierly conduct'. By September 1944 when the embattled and beleagured British 1st Airborne Division's commander General Frost contemplated surrendering to the Waffen-SS he remembers saying to someone 'I don't think this is going to be much of a pleasure! We had all heard stories of them [the SS] shooting their prisoners and herding them into burning buildings', but later he was relieved to discover that these Waffen-SS men were 'kind, chivalrous and even comforting' to their British captives.

The deeper and deeper the Allies penetrated into Germany the more Waffen-SS prisoners they took, and these were usually treated in much the same way as other German PoWs. But when the British liberated Belsen Concentration Camp they became, according to a war correspondent who was present, 'full of a cold fury so intense that it was unbearable even to talk to them'. Thereafter all SS men, young or old, officer or man, conscript or volunteer were treated as war criminals with varying degrees of harshness and brutality. As the war's end became a matter of days, Allied soldiers didn't take kindly to what they considered futile resistance. The killing of one of their comrades by SS 'last-ditchers' was repaid with interest, and particularly in the very last days of the war SS men who resisted and then surrendered were lucky to be taken prisoner at all. The vengeance of liberated concentration camp inmates and forced labourers fell on those SS men who were taken prisoner in the vicinity of the camp. But in Dachau for example the regular guards fled shortly before the arrival of the Americans and their places had been taken by Waffen-SS conscripts from a nearby training unit.

The indescribable chaos of a destroyed and defeated nation placed an enormous burden on the Allied forces of occupation. The country was like an ant hill which had been kicked apart and it swarmed with soldiers, displaced persons and evacuees. From the East poured the battered remnants of the once mighty Waffen-SS, their few vehicles no longer bristling with machine guns, but festooned with evacuees and their pitiful belongings. Travelling eastwards along the same roads were millions of forced labourers, Soviet prisoners of war and concentration camp survivors. They passed each other in silent columns both too pre-occupied with the uncertainty of the future to take much notice of each other.

All over Germany vast reception centres were set up for the estimated seven million prisoners and disarmed military personnel. These were not always camps in the accepted sense, often fields with no shelter and no fences. Soldiers dug themselves shallow grave-like trenches and slept in them covered by a greatcoat or blanket. Lucky for them it was the beginning of summer. Food was desperately short and if it hadn't been for the generosity of the civilians who shared their own meagre rations with their menfolk, many would have died of hunger. But these were the lucky ones when one considers the fate of their comrades who fell into the hands of the Czechs or Yugoslavs. It is impossible to say how many Germans – soldiers and civilians – fell victim to the vengeance of the victors, but it is estimated that at least two million Germans died after the capitulation on 8 May 1945.

The main Allied priority was to get Germany back on its feet again as far as possible before the coming of winter. The first categories of prisoners, those in agriculture and mining, were screened, given identity papers and ration cards and released, but if during this process membership of the SS came to light the prisoner was sent to a special camp, where special teams of American CIC (Criminal Intelligence Corps) and British CIS (Counter Intelligence Service) officers searched for those whose names appeared on wanted lists of war criminals. Wolff Sendele ended up in such a camp with 10,000 other SS men in which there was a compound holding about 250 suspected war criminals.

Richard Schulze-Kossens was taken prisoner on 29 April 1945 when his division surrendered to the Americans, 'I was then sent to thirteen different camps where in all honesty I must say the prisoners were badly treated. I was beaten. I was handcuffed, put into a jeep and taken twice to Nuremberg as a defence witness. During our first year of imprisonment the treatment was so bad that it didn't conform to the Geneva Convention. Bearing in mind that we had been taken prisoner in Germany it was only after five months that we were allowed to write to our families. Half the camp was undernourished and I had to start a hunger strike. I think we were subjected to special treatment, because the Americans thought we were the hard cases, but in 1946–1947 things began to get better.'

The Geneva Convention limits the amount of time and the circumstances in which prisoners of war can be detained, and so the Allies were obliged to transfer prisoners of war to the status of civilian internees and prisoner of war camps became internment camps in June 1946.

The SS was not very strongly represented at the first session of the International Military Tribunal which began in the Palace of Justice in Nuremberg in October 1946. Of the twenty defendants only two were full SS members, and four others honorary members of the SS. But in this first tribunal five groups – the Reich cabinet, the Leadership Corps of the NSDAP, the SS and SD, the Gestapo, and the High Command of the German Armed Forces were indicted as criminal organizations. The two SS defendants Ernst Kaltenbrunner, Heydrich's successor as chief of the Reich Security Main Office and Arthur Seyss Inquart were both found guilty and hanged. The tribunal also declared the SS and all its offices, departments, services, agencies, branches, formations, organizations and groups, including the SD and the Gestapo, to be a criminal organization. This meant that 'members will be subject to trial and punishment on account of their membership in accordance with the provisions of the Charter of this Tribunal and upon any such trial the criminal character of the groups or organization shall be considered proved and shall not be questioned'.

During 1946 and 1947 further trials of the SS departments responsible for medicine, racial matters, justice, the concentration camps and the *Einsatzgruppen* with a total of 96 defendants, nearly all of whom were SS members, took place. At the same time other trials of SS personnel were being held in the British occupation zone. The American trials took place in Dachau which had become a huge prison holding 32,000 former SS men. As a touch of bitter irony Landsberg Prison, where Hitler had been imprisoned after the November 1923 putsch, was chosen as the place of execution for those sentenced to death. Following sentencing in the courts of the Western Allies, a number of convicted war criminals were extradited to Poland and elsewhere, and again stood trial.

By 1948 most Waffen-SS men who had been accused of committing war crimes had been released by the Western Allies. This was due in part to the intensification of the Cold War which led to a new Allied attitude to Western Germany. In May 1949 the German Federal Republic came into being and one of its first acts was to restore diplomatic relations with the Soviet Union which led to the release of the remaining German prisoners of war in Soviet captivity including many former Waffen-SS men. Despite being an anti-Nazi the first Chancellor Conrad Adenauer campaigned for the release of all remaining war criminals still in prison in Germany, but it was not until 1956 that the last of the 'red jackets' of Landsberg who had had their death sentences quashed were released.

As a new democratic Germany emerged from the rubble and embarked on its economic recovery former SS men began to re-integrate themselves into German society. At first they took whatever jobs they could get, but there were two groups whose particular skills were in as much demand after the war as during it. In the early 1950s those officials of the SD and Gestapo with knowledge of conditions inside the Soviet Union were taken into the intelligence service of the German Federal Republic. When its chief, the former General Staff officer Reinhard Gehlen, was obliged to answer criticism that between one and five per cent of his staff were former SS men, Gehlen replied that if he didn't give them a job they would be snapped up by the East German State Security Service, which he maintained was largely staffed by ex-SS men.

Equally tainted by a Nazi past, but also indispensible were Germany's policemen. Although the Allies were supposed to have de-Nazified the German police at the end of the war, many Nazi officials resumed their police careers in the 1950s. In order not to undermine the public's confidence in its police force there has always been a marked reluctance to expose the wartime activities of its policemen.

In many ways the 1950s were good years for former Nazis and SS men in the German Federal Republic. Article 131 of the constitution removed the ban on former Nazis serving in the civil service. The Allied war crimes trials had come to an end, and German courts were not yet empowered to try Germans for crimes committed in the formerly occupied territories. By the end of the 1960s and at the height of the German economic miracle former Nazis in the 45 to 60 age group represented 65 to 70 per cent of all top managerial posts with graduates of the Adolf Hitler Schools and former Waffen-SS people in the lead.

But at the same time a new generation of Germans was beginning to make its voice heard. Freed from the restraint imposed by complicity they demanded that Germany could only overcome its past and gain the respect of the world at large if those guilty of terrible crimes during the Third Reich did not go unpunished.

The main problem facing German courts was that they could only bring charges for crimes committed within the Federal jurisdiction of a particular *Land*, whereas most of the crimes had been committed on foreign territory. To overcome this legal loophole a special Justice Department was established at Ludwigsburg for the systematic investigation of Nazi crimes wherever they were committed. Since its opening in 1958 this department has conducted over 12,000 investigations which have resulted in over 6,500 convictions. It is estimated that since the end of the war a total of 50,000

119

Germans have been convicted of Nazi crimes by German and foreign courts.

Despite the repeated extension of the Statute of Limitations today a former SS man can only be charged with the crime of murder or accessory to murder, and he can only be found guilty if it can be proved, as in any other criminal case, that he personally killed someone or helped in the killing of someone.

Of course there are people who think that so long after the war such terrible acts should be forgotten, and the elderly defendants should be left in peace to live out their remaining years. But it has also sunk into the consciousness of many that they are not on trial as SS men but as criminals. Even by wartime standards the crimes they have been accused of were particularly ghastly. By their behaviour they had shown that they fully identified themselves with the murderous regime which they served, and none of them had been *ordered* to carry out the sadistic crimes with which they are charged.

Considering the extent of their crimes and the number of their victims, the SS as a whole got off remarkably lightly, and yet they refuse to accept the verdict of history, which holds the SS responsible for the extermination of the Jews. Although the Nuremberg condemnation of the SS as a criminal organization has no legal significance it still causes great resentment amongst a group of Germans who as young Waffen-SS men gave their all to the Fatherland. They are today paying the penalty for their lack of circumspection. As in all great tragedies there is always more than one victim, and in the case of the SS there are probably more victims than in any other tragedy, and that includes the surviving SS men themselves.

Appendix I

The Thames Television documentary *SS 1923–1945* and this publication include extracts of interviews with the following people;

Sir George Kennard Born 27 April 1915, regular Army officer and one-time ADC to General Wavell. Captured during Greek Campaign by the *Leibstandarte SS Adolf Hitler*. After the war commanded 4th King's Own Hussars. Retired 1958.

Hermann Langbein Born in 1912 in Vienna. Served in International Brigade in Civil War. Interned in France until transferred by Germans to Dachau, and then in 1942 to Auschwitz. After liberation became Secretary of the *Comité International des Camps*. Author of a number of books about Auschwitz.

Heiner Lichtenstein Born Chemnitz in 1932. Editor *West Deutsche Rundfunk* in Cologne, in which capacity he has observed and written about a number of Nazi war crime trials.

Dr Jur Adalbert Rückerl Since 1958 director of the Central Office for the Investigation of National Socialist Crimes based in Ludwigsburg.

Wolf Sendele Born 1916 in Vienna. Joined SS in February 1932. 1933 transferred to Political Readiness Squad Wurttemburg. Dismissed 1934. Served in German Army during World War II and interned for eighteen months after war because of his SS membership.

Richard Schulze (*-Kossens*) Born 1914 in Berlin as eldest son of regular Prussian Army officer. Joined SS in 1934 and graduated from SS officers' academy in 1936. Seconded to Foreign Office and accompanied Ribbentrop to Moscow for the signing of German–Soviet Pact. Fought with *Leibstandarte SS Adolf Hitler* in campaigns of 1939, 1940 and 1941. In October 1941 appointed to Hitler's staff. Captured at the end of the War by the Americans. Today lives in retirement in Düsseldorf.

Alfred Spiess Born 12 October 1919. In 1938 joined Air Force and served until 1944 in Anti-Aircraft Artillery. After release from US prisoner of war camp studied law and qualified in 1953. From 1964 involved in Treblinka Trial. At present Leading Senior State Prosecutor in Wuppertal.

Hans Wissebach Born October 1919 as sixth child of a labourer. Joined *SS-Verfügungstruppe* in 1937. Fought with *SS-Totenkopf* Division in Russia until wounded and blinded in March 1942. Taken prisoner by the Red Army he did not return to Germany until 1956. Went into politics and today is CDU member of Parliament in the Bundeshaus.

Karl Wolff Born Darmstadt in May 1900. April 1917 until end of World War I served in Hessian Life Guard Infantry Regiment. Joined SS in October 1931 and in May 1933 became Himmler's personal adjutant. In 1939 appointed Himmler's liaison officer in the *Führer* headquarters. In 1943 Supreme SS and Police Leader in Italy and negotiated capitulation on 29 April 1945. Released 1951, rearrested 1962 and sentenced in Munich to fifteen years hard labour in 1964. Since 1975 living in retirement in Darmstadt.

Appendix II

HIMMLER (*Reichsführer-SS*)
WOLFF (*Chef des Persönlichen-Stabes RF-SS*)
BERGER (*SS-Hauptamt*)

	HANS JÜTTNER (*SS-Führungshauptamt*)	OSWALD POHL (*SS-Wirtschafts-Verwaltungshauptamt*)	REINHARD HEYDRICH (*Reichssicherheitshauptamt*)	KURT DALUEGE (*Hauptamt Ordnungspolizei*)
			Supreme and Senior SS and Police Commanders to co-ordinate the activities of the security forces under Himmler's control	
REICH	*Waffen-SS* *Allgemeine-SS*	Concentration camps and economic enterprises employing camp labour	Inspector of Security Police and SD (IdS) controlling *Gestapo*, Criminal Police and SD offices and outstations	Inspector of Police (IdO) controlling district and local police
OCCUPIED AREAS	*Waffen-SS* garrisons and training areas etc. *Allgemeine-SS* in incorporated territories *Germanische-SS* in 'Germanic' countries	Concentration camps (including extermination facilities at Auschwitz and Majdanek) and economic enterprises employing camp and ghetto labour	*Befehlshaber* of Security Police and SD (BdS) controlling a number of commanders of Sipo and SD (KdS) and a network of outstations. Also extermination and labour camps and ghettos.	Commander of Police (BdO) controlling police units (*Truppenverbände*) organised in regiments, battalions and companies
INVADED AREAS	*Waffen-SS* field formations under *Wehrmacht* control. *Kommandostab RF-SS* commanding Waffen-SS troops under Himmler's control		*Einsatzgruppen* each composed of a number of *Einsatzkommandos* and *Sonderkommandos*	Police formations and units controlled by SS or *Wehrmacht* for security duties behind the front

Select Bibliography

ARONSON, Shlomo, *Reinhard Heydrich und die Frügeschichte von Gestapo und SD*. Deutsche Verlags-Anstalt, Stuttgart, 1971.

ARONSON, Shlomo, *The Beginnings of the Gestapo System*. Israel Universities Press, Jerusalem, 1969.

BLEUEL, Hans Peter, *Sex and Society in Nazi Germany*. J. B. Lippincott Company, Philadelphia and New York, 1971.

DALLIN, Alexander, *German Rule in Russia 1941–1945*. Macmillan & Co Ltd, London, 1957.

D'ALQUEN, Gunter, *Die SS, Geschichte, Aufgabe und Organisation der Schutzstaffeln der NSDAP*. Junker und Dünnhaupt Verlag, Berlin, 1939.

DEMANT, Ebbo, *Auschwitz – 'Direkt von der Rampe weg ...'*. Rowohlt Taschenbuch Verlag GmbH, Reinbek bei Hamburg, March, 1979.

DESCHNER, Günther, *Reinhard Heydrich Statthalter der totalen Macht*. Wilhelm Heyne Verlag, Munich, 1977.

FEST, Joachim C., *The Face of the Third Reich*. Penguin Books Ltd, Harmondsworth, England, 1972.

GRUNBERGER, Richard, *A Social History of the Third Reich*. Penguin Books Ltd, Harmondsworth, England, 1974.

HAUSSER, Paul, *Soldaten wie andere auch*. Munin Verlag GmbH, Osnabrück, 1966.

HILBERG, Raul, *The Destruction of the European Jews*. Quadrangle Books Inc., Chicago, 1961.

HILLEL, Clarissa, Henry and Marc, *Children of the SS*. Transworld Publishers Ltd, London, 1977.

HOFFMANN, Peter, *Hitler's Personal Security*. The Macmillan Press Ltd, London and Basingstoke, 1979.

HÖHNE, Heinz, *The Order of the Death's Head*. Secker & Warburg London, 1969.

HÖSS, Rudolf, *Commandant of Auschwitz*. Pan Books Ltd, London, 1961.

KLIETMANN, Dr Kurt G., *Die Waffen-SS eine Dokumentation*. Verlag 'Der Freiwillige' GmbH, Osnabrück, 1965.

Konzentrationslager Dachau 1933–1945. Comité International de Dachau, Brussels, 1965.

KRAUSNICK, H., BUCHHEIM, H., BROSZAT, M. and JACOBSEN, Hans-Adolf, *Anatomy of the SS State*. William Collins Sons and Company Ltd, London, 1968.

LICHTENSTEIN, Heiner, *Majdanek*. Europäische Verlagsanstalt, Frankfurt am Main, 1979.

MARSALEK, Hans, *Die Geschichte des Konzentrationslagers Mauthausen*. Österreichische Lagergemeinschaft Mauthausen, Vienna, 1980.

MOLLO, Andrew, *A Pictorial History of the SS 1923–1945*. Macdonald and Jane's, London, 1976.

REITLINGER, Gerald, *The Final Solution*. Sphere Books Ltd, London 1971.

SAUER, Karl, *Die Verbrechen der Waffen-SS*. Röderberg-Verlag, Frankfurt am Main, 1977.

SCHELLENBERG, Walter, *The Schellenberg Memoirs*. Andre Deutsch Ltd, 1956.

SERENY, Gitta, *Into That Darkness*. Pan Books Ltd, London, 1977.

SPEER, Albert, *Inside the Third Reich*. Weidenfeld and Nicolson, London, 1970.

STEIN, George H., *The Waffen-SS, Hitler's Elite Guard at War 1939–1945*. Oxford University Press, London, 1966.

SHIRER, William L., *The Rise and Fall of the Third Reich*. Secker and Warburg Ltd, London, 1960.

SYDNOR, Charles W. Jr., *Soldiers of Destruction, The SS Death's Head Division 1933–1945*. Princeton University Press, New Jersey, 1977.

TREVOR-ROPER, H. R., *The Last Days of Hitler*. Macmillan & Co Ltd, London, 1962.

TREVOR-ROPER, H. R., *Hitler's Table Talk 1941–1944*. Weidenfeld & Nicolson, London, 1973.

WEGNER, Bernd, *Das Führerkorps der Bewaffneten SS, 1933–1945*. Dissertation for Doctorate of Philosophy at the University of Hamburg, 1977.

WEINGARTNER, J., *The Leibstandarte Adolf Hitler 1933–1945*. Thesis for Doctorate of Philosophy at the University of Wisconsin, 1967.

Index

128